BRITISH STRATIGRAPHY

F. A. Middlemiss, BSc PhD

Emeritus Reader in Geology in the
University of London

SECOND EDITION

London
ALLEN & UNWIN
Boston   Sydney

Allen & Unwin (Publishers) Ltd,
40 Museum Street, London WC1A 1LU, UK

Allen & Unwin (Publishers) Ltd,
Park Lane, Hemel Hempstead, Herts HP2 4TE, UK

Allen & Unwin Inc.,
8 Winchester Place, Winchester, Mass. 01890, USA

Allen & Unwin Australia Pty Ltd.,
8 Napier Street, North Sydney, NSW 2060, Australia

First published in 1969
Second edition, 1986

Photographs on pages 12, 25, 29, 34 and 38 were kindly supplied by,
and reproduced by permission of, the British Geological Survey.

British Library Cataloguing in Publication Data

Middlemiss, F. A.
    British stratigraphy.—2nd ed.—(Introducing geology; v. 2)
    1. Geology—Great Britain   2. Geology, Stratigraphic
    I. Title   II. Series
    551.7′00941   QE261
    ISBN 0-04-550034-7

Set in 10 on 11 point Times by
Mathematical Composition Setters Ltd, Salisbury, UK
and printed in Great Britain by
Thetford Press, Thetford, Norfolk

27 FEB

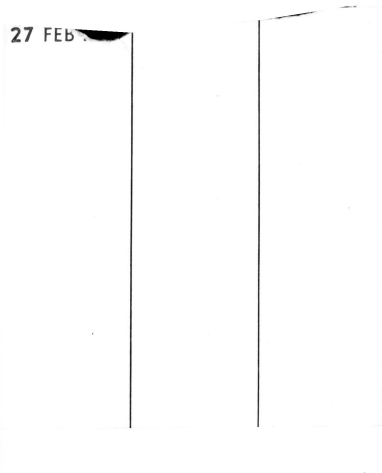

Preface to the First Edition

This book is primarily intended to assist candidates studying geology for the Ordinary Level of GCE, and examinations of comparable standard, but it should also be found useful by the reader requiring a rapid conspectus of the geological history of Britain, and as forming a basis for more advanced work. The scope of the subject matter necessitated a narrow and slippery path between over-simplification and excessive detail, but the balance adopted is based upon the experience of many years of teaching at all levels, and of examining for the London GCE Board. The maps, combining outcrop distribution with palaeogeography, presented some difficulty, especially for periods of continuously changing geography, such as the Cretaceous. It was necessary in these cases to make an arbitrary choice of one small part of the period, the geography of which could be illustrated. Candidates are advised not to spend time learning every detail of the out-crop patterns, but to concentrate upon the main areas of outcrop.

I am indebted to Mrs Jean Fyffe for the cartographic work.

F. A. MIDDLEMISS
Queen Mary College, University of London, 1969

Preface to the Revised Metric Edition

The opportunity has been taken of eradicating a few minor errors, one of which was kindly pointed out by a correspondent. Cognisance has also been taken of recently published isotopic dating results. The main change, however, has been occasioned by the general acceptance of the theory of plate tectonics, which I have attempted to summarise very briefly, in so far as it is relevant, in Chapter 3.

F. A. MIDDLEMISS
Queen Mary College, University of London, 1973

Preface to the Second Edition

I am grateful to many correspondents for their suggested improvements, most of which have been incorporated. Both text and figures have been expanded to allow greater attention to be given to faunal and floral content of the rocks, and to palaeogeography and plate movements.

F. A. MIDDLEMISS
Queen Mary College, Universtiy of London, 1984

Contents

Chapter 1

Geological history

Stratigraphy is the study of the history of rocks – their sequence in time, their distribution, their varying types and structures. The word 'stratigraphy' is derived from the word 'strata', meaning layers of sedimentary rocks (also called beds). Strictly speaking, the term 'historical geology' should be applied to a study which includes the history of igneous and metamorphic rocks. But, as the succession of sedimentary strata provides such a convenient natural chronological table into which all events during geological time can be fitted, the word 'stratigraphy' is usually taken to mean the whole historical aspect of geology.

Stratigraphy is not a branch of geology on its own, rather a drawing together of all the branches of the subject to fulfil what has been defined as the main aim of geology: to trace the evolution of the crust of the Earth and of life upon it. In order to do this, stratigraphy draws upon the following four main branches of geology:

(1) The study of the materials (rocks and minerals) of which the Earth is made – this forms **petrology** and **mineralogy**.
(2) The study of the physical processes which have affected these materials, both within the Earth and upon its surface – this is included in **physical** and **structural** geology.
(3) **Palaeontology** – the study of the development of life on Earth as shown by fossil remains.
(4) The study of the distribution, both in space and time, of all these materials, processes and forms of life.

Obviously all these branches of study are needed to contribute to the working out of what has happened to the Earth during geological time, but it is the study of **distribution** which enables all the other studies to be put into a historical framework, as it enables us to see the inter-relationships between the materials that were formed, the processes that went on and the creatures that lived at the time.

The study of stratigraphy – taken to include the relationships which strata have to one another,

structural changes (such as plate tectonics and the occurrence of folding and faulting), the extrusion and intrusion of igneous rocks, and metamorphism – gives an insight into the history of the planet on which we live, and helps the understanding of the economic aspect of geology: the history of rocks containing oil or mineral ores can provide important clues to their present-day spatial distribution.

Fundamental laws of stratigraphy

The first essential in any attempt to work out geological history (that is to put geological events into their correct chronological order) is to find out the order of deposition of the strata (beds), and the chief clues to this are contained in a few fundamental laws (Fig. 1):

(1) **The Law of Superposition** This is the apparently rather obvious rule that if one stratum lies on top of another then the upper stratum is the *younger*. Sedimentary strata are, of course, deposited in succession, with younger on top of older, but the application of the law is obvious only when the original order has not been disturbed by later events.
(2) **The Law of Contained Fragments** If eroded fragments of one rock are contained in another then the rock containing the fragments is the *younger*.
(3) **The Law of Intrusive Junctions** If an igneous rock has been intruded into a sedimentary stratum, or into another igneous rock, then the intruded rock must be the *younger*.
(4) **Sedimentary structures** Any structure imparted to a rock during deposition or soon after, while the material was still soft, which has a clear directional element with respect to gravity, may indicate the original 'way up' of the beds and hence the order of age. Examples of this are the foreset beds of cross-bedding, (see Fig. 24, p. 30) and contemporaneous animal burrows which let sediment from one stratum down into another.

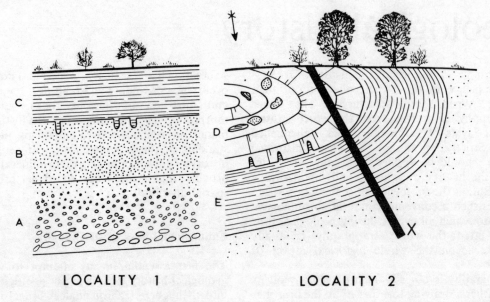

LOCALITY 1   LOCALITY 2

Figure 1 Some fundamental laws of stratigraphy
At locality 1, the strata are in their original order. C must be younger than B, and B younger than A (law of super-position). A exhibits graded bedding (coarsest at the bottom). The top of bed B is penetrated by the burrows of animals which lived on the sea floor at the time. At locality 2 the beds have been overfolded and are upside down, except immediately beneath the arrow, where they are still in their original order. The inversion of E and D is shown by the direction of the burrows; D is older than E. D contains fragments of beds B and C, seen at locality 1, and hence must be younger than they (law of contained fragments). The dyke X cuts across D and E and so must be younger than those beds.

Correlating rocks of the same age

Since only a few strata at the most can be exposed at any one place and time, it is very important to know whether the particular rocks one is examining are of the same age, or older, or younger than those somewhere else. In other words, it is important to be able to correlate the rocks in one place with those in another. One obvious method of doing this is by seeing whether they are of the same kind of rock, that is, by using the method of **lithological similarity** (from the Greek word *lithos* meaning stone). This method has to be relied upon sometimes but it is very unsatisfactory since similar kinds of rock have been formed at very different times, and conversely the rocks formed at any given time in the Earth's history may vary rapidly from place to place. An example of this is the group of strata called the Corallian Beds in England, all deposited within one relatively short period of geological time. Around Oxford they consist mainly of limestones, including fossil coral

reefs, and sands, whereas in Buckinghamshire they are entirely clays. Within a few miles, the overall character (or **facies**) of the group of strata has changed completely owing to the difference in their conditions of deposition in the two areas.

The more reliable method of correlation is by means of the fossils contained in the beds (Fig. 2). It was first realised at the end of the 18th century by William Smith that each group of strata contained a distinctive assemblage of fossils, which not only characterised that group and no other, but also was present in that group wherever it occurred, and so could be used to identify it. To a large extent this is true in spite of even drastic changes of facies, particularly with certain types of fossils. In the case of the Corallian Beds, for example, the same ammonites can be found in both the calcareous and the clayey facies. Such fossils can be called **index fossils**.

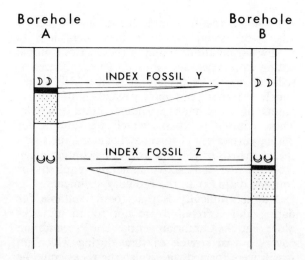

Borehole A   Borehole B

INDEX FOSSIL Y

INDEX FOSSIL Z

Figure 2   Correlation by fossils
The coal seam and sandstone encountered in borehole A might be thought the same as those encountered in borehole B, but the occurrence of the two different index fossils shows them to be of different ages.

Unconformities

In some sequences of stratified sedimentary rocks a great thickness of beds lies regularly one upon another, showing that sedimentation continued more or less regularly for a long period of time; such a sequence is said to be **conformable**. Sometimes, however, it is found that the base of a sequence of strata rests upon the eroded edges of an obviously older group of strata, the dip and strike of which may be quite different from that of the overlying beds (see Fig. 17, p. 21). This is a case of **unconformity**. Unconformity is a very important phenomenon since it gives evidence of major events in the geological history of the area. It tells us three things about the older group of strata: that they have been (a) folded or faulted, or both; (b) uplifted; and (c) eroded *before* the younger strata were deposited upon their truncated edges. Another noteworthy law arising from this is that any folding or faulting must be *younger* than the youngest rock it affects.

The stratigraphical column

By applying these laws, geologists have been able to arrange the rocks of the Earth's crust in chronological order and also to group them into divisions of time called **eras**, each one sub-divided into **periods**. Originally the boundaries between these were decided largely by the presence of unconformities, but no unconformity is so widespread as to be found everywhere, and the

time period represented by an unconformity in one place may be represented by a conformable succession in another. The boundaries are now drawn on the evidence of the fossils present, each era and period having, in general, its own characteristic assemblage of fossils. If rocks laid down during all these eras and periods were found in one place they would constitute an ideal **stratigraphical** (or geological) **column** (Fig. 3). In fact, of course, there is no place on Earth where the column is complete; everywhere there are gaps, large or small, represented by unconformities or by periods when no sediment was deposited at that particular place, or, if deposited was soon eroded again. This emphasises again the importance of correlation. Note that the name used for each of the eras and periods refers both to that stretch of time and to the actual rocks formed during that time. The rocks formed during a period constitute a **system**; thus the Cambrian system of rocks was formed during Cambrian time.

Isotopic dating

The absolute age of rocks in years can be worked out approximately by the methods of isotopic dating. These depend upon analysis of radioactive minerals which are known to change in chemical composition with time at a uniform rate. Such methods are difficult to apply, especially to

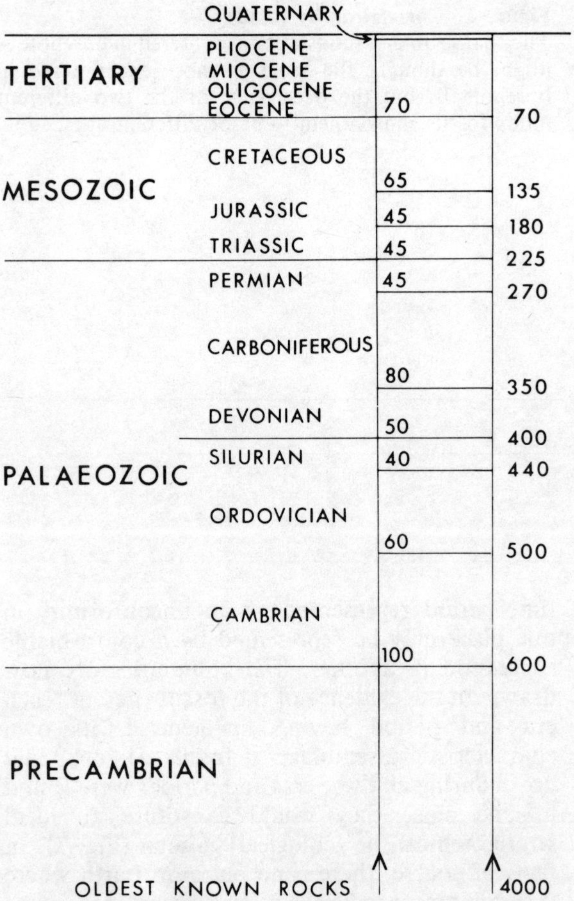

	QUATERNARY		
TERTIARY	PLIOCENE		
	MIOCENE		
	OLIGOCENE		
	EOCENE	70	70
MESOZOIC	CRETACEOUS	65	135
	JURASSIC	45	180
	TRIASSIC	45	225
	PERMIAN	45	270
	CARBONIFEROUS	80	350
	DEVONIAN	50	400
PALAEOZOIC	SILURIAN	40	440
	ORDOVICIAN	60	500
	CAMBRIAN	100	600
PRECAMBRIAN			
OLDEST KNOWN ROCKS			4000

Figure 3 The stratigraphical column
The eras are named in the left-hand column, the periods in the centre column. The figures in the centre give the duration of each period in millions of years, those on the right record the number of millions of years measured back from the present-day.

sedimentary rocks, in which radioactive minerals do not often occur in sufficient quantity. Most of the isotopic dates worked out for sedimentary strata are based only upon analyses of associated igneous rocks. For detailed correlation of fossiliferous strata, suitable fossils give much more accurate dating than isotopic methods as so far developed, but dating by fossils is, of course, relative and cannot be stated in terms of 'years ago'.

However, in many parts of the world there are important groups of sedimentary rocks which do not contain fossils suitable for dating (especially where the sediments have been deposited in freshwater conditions) and in these cases isotopic dating can sometimes be used. The sequences of sedimentary rocks in the East African Rift Valley which in recent years have yielded significant remains of early man provide a good example. These contain no fossils which are suitable for dating purposes, but fortunately among the strata there are beds of volcanic ash which contain much more of the radioactive minerals required for isotopic dating than the ordinary sediments.

Another difficulty is that fossils suitable for dating and correlation are not found in rocks older than the Cambrian period. The Precambrian covers a vast stretch of time during which no fossils were formed with which the rocks could be correlated. Some interesting fossils have been found in the younger Precambrian rocks, but it remains generally true to say that there are none of stratigraphical value. Isotopic dating is therefore of great importance and most correlation of Precambrian rocks is based upon it, especially as the majority of these old rocks have been metamorphosed and so contain abundant minerals suitable for isotopic analysis, such as biotite mica, or are cut by numerous igneous intrusions and mineral veins containing such minerals.

Geological time

The extent of geological time, that is of time since the Earth was formed, is so enormous compared with the human timescale that it is difficult to grasp. A vivid way of comprehending the geological timescale is to imagine all the time since the Earth's beginning as the 24 hours of a day (Fig. 4). Then, if the Earth was formed at one minute past midnight, the earliest fossils useful for correlation (at the beginning of the Cambrian) lived at about 8.30 the following evening, the earliest land plants and freshwater fishes about an hour later. The first reptiles evolved soon after 10 p.m. and the first mammals at about 10.50. The dinosaurs flourished on the Earth from about 11 p.m. to 11. 35. The first human beings appeared at about two minutes to midnight, and the whole of recorded human history occupies about the last one and a half seconds.

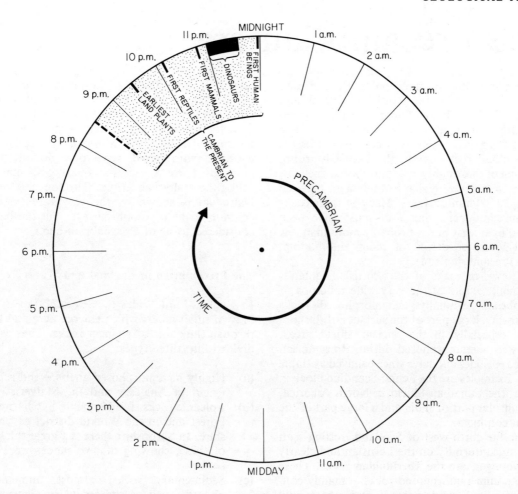

Figure 4 Geological timescales
Imagine the Earth's history compressed into one day. If the Earth was formed at one minute past midnight, then the first life to become part of the fossil record did not appear until after eight o'clock in the evening, and human beings have inhabited the Earth for just the two minutes before midnight.

The maps illustrating the following chapters have been drawn on an outline of the British Isles so as to relate ancient geography to the places we know. However, it must be remembered that the present familiar shape of the coastlines is something very modern, dating only from quite late in the Pleistocene, perhaps three seconds before midnight on the clock. Maps showing the coastlines as they were in earlier geological periods would be quite unrecognisable as Britain.

Chapter 2

The Precambrian era

The largest areas of outcropping Precambrian rocks in Britain are in the Scottish Highlands and Northern Ireland. In the Outer Hebrides and on the Scottish mainland north-west of a distinct line running from near Cape Wrath to Skye (Fig. 5) are the oldest rocks of all, the **Lewisian** group, consisting of thoroughly metamorphosed gneisses, schists and marbles, giving isotopic ages between 2600 and 1100 million years. Many of these rocks were once sediments but they must have been involved in at least one – probably more than one – **orogenesis**, or period of mountain-building, during Precambrian time.

The Lewisian rocks of the Scottish Highlands are a small sample of the very wide outcrops of Precambrian regionally metamorphosed rocks which form a large part of the surfaces of the continents, especially in the ancient shield areas, which were metamorphosed during Precambrian orogenic episodes and have since behaved as stable blocks. Examples are the Fenno-Scandian block in Europe, the Canadian Shield in North America, the peninsular part of India and a large part of the African continent.

In the far north-west of Scotland, resting with violent unconformity on the Lewisian and clearly much younger, are the **Torridonian** rocks. These are quite unmetamorphosed rocks – mainly conglomerates and sandstones – and one would hardly think them as old as Precambrian if they were not themselves overlain unconformably by the Cambrian. These dramatic relationships are clearly shown on the north shore of Loch Assynt in north-west Scotland (Figs 6 and 7). From the Cape Wrath – Skye line southeastwards to the middle of the Grampian Highlands, a group of Precambrian metamorphic rocks called the Moine or **Moinian** group outcrops. These rocks are probably, although not certainly, of the same age as the Torridonian, and if so present a significant contrast. The Moine rocks were highly metamor-

phosed around the end of Lower Palaeozoic time (pp. 9–13), whereas the Torridonian rocks have remained completely unmetamorphosed.

In the southern and eastern Highlands and in northern Ireland, the Moinian is overlain by another, more varied, series of regionally metamorphosed rocks (schists, quartzites, marbles) called the **Dalradian** group. The top part of the Dalradian is shown by the very rare fossils it contains to be of Cambrian age, but the base is considered to be of Precambrian age.

The Precambrian in England and Wales

In England and Wales the Precambrian is seen only in small inliers which emerge here and there through the cover of younger rocks. They can be divided into three types:

(a) Highly metamorphosed gneisses and schists, found in Anglesey and the Malvern Hills.
(b) Volcanic rocks, found mainly in Charnwood Forest and in the Wrekin district of Shropshire. In Shropshire there is a great thickness of these, showing that volcanoes were very active.
(c) Sedimentary rocks, almost unmetamorphosed, such as are found in Charnwood Forest, and especially in the Longmynd of Shropshire, where they are some 6150 metres thick.

The volcanic and sedimentary types are closely associated with each other and both are certainly of late Precambrian age, yet in Shropshire the evidence is clear that they have been involved in large-scale folding and profound erosion *before* the Cambrian was laid unconformably upon them.

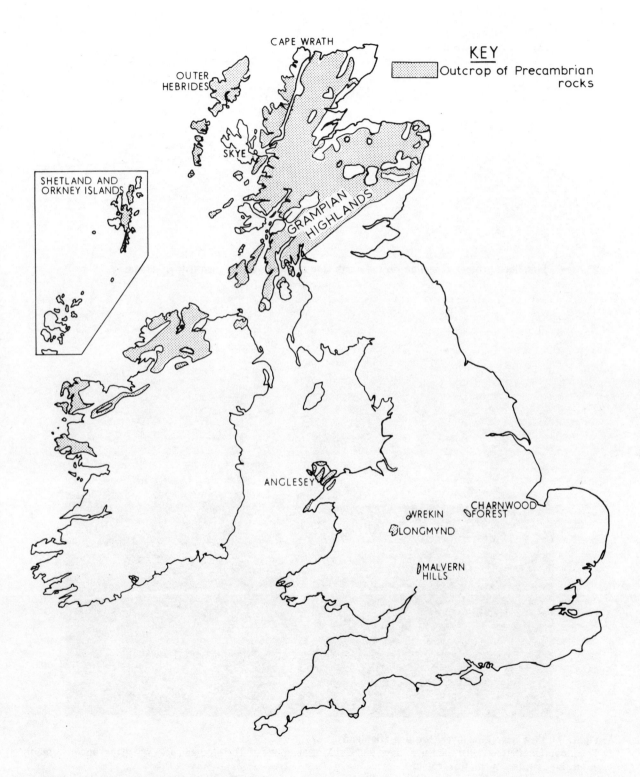

Figure 5   Outcrops of Precambrian rocks

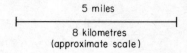

5 miles

8 kilometres
(approximate scale)

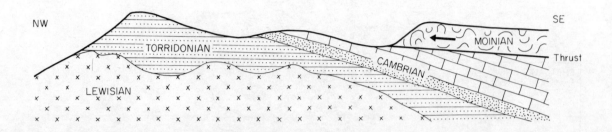

NW

TORRIDONIAN

LEWISIAN

CAMBRIAN

MOINIAN

Thrust

SE

Figure 6   Simplified geological section on the north side of Loch Assynt, Scottish Highlands

Figure 7   View near Lochinver, Scottish Highlands
The mountains (left to right) Canisp, Suilven and Cul Mor are made of Torridonian rocks which rest unconformably upon the Lewisian in the foreground.

The Lower Palaeozoic geosyncline

The principal interest of the Lower Palaeozoic era in the British area lies in the development of a **geosyncline** which later became transformed by major folding movements into a folded mountain chain. A geosyncline can be defined as an elongated downwarping of the crust of the Earth, forming a deep trough in which a great thickness of sediments accumulates (Fig. 8). This definition needs to be enlarged upon somewhat. Firstly, the downwarp is occupied by the sea and the environment of sedimentation is normally marine. Secondly, sedimentation may, or may not, keep pace with the downwarping – the sediments being therefore of shallow-water type in the former case but of deep-water type in the second. Thirdly, an essential part of the definition is that the geosynclinal sediments are later compressed and folded by the movement together of the sides of the downwarp, and so come to form fold-mountains.

Plate movements and the geosyncline

What causes a geosyncline to develop is uncertain. Those which have formed in different parts of the world during geological time differ considerably one from another in detail, and it may be that there is no one mechanism of formation to which all can be attributed. Most geosynclines, at least of those that developed since late Precambrian times, are thought to represent the zone where one of the major plates of the Earth's crust is diving beneath the edge of another such plate, thus dragging down the crust and forming an elongated downwarp (Fig. 8). Many geologists therefore believe that the Lower Palaeozoic geosyncline in the British area represented, at the beginning of the era, quite a wide ocean, called 'Iapetus', between a 'European' plate to the south-east and an 'American' plate to the north-west (Figs 9 and 8a). During the Lower Palaeozoic, according to this theory, the European plate slipped progressively under the American plate (a process called **subduction**), so that the two continents approached closer and closer to each other, the downwarp (geosyncline) between them becoming steadily filled with sediments eroded from both sides.

Finally, by the end of the era, the two continents had become joined together, the sediments of the geosyncline squeezed and uplifted to form a folded mountain chain (Fig. 8a). If the diagram is applied to the Lower Palaeozoic of Britain it would represent a fairly late stage in this process (about late Ordovician), when the approach of the crustal plates had already made Iapetus quite narrow. At this stage the earlier sediments had, in fact, already been folded by previous subduction.

Rock types formed in the geosyncline

The most typical sedimentary rocks of the geosynclinal environment are the **greywackes**. These are ill-sorted sandstones which represent rapid deposition in the subsiding geosynclinal basin; they are essentially sediments which have been 'poured in' to the geosyncline and usually occur in great thicknesses. In the central parts of the geosyncline one would expect to find fine-grained sediments, consisting partly of the finest material which has been carried farthest, partly of fine organic debris or volcanic dust which has dropped from the surface waters. Another important factor is that the passage of one crustal plate beneath another releases vast quantities of heat energy and leads to the uprise of igneous magma from below. Thus there are usually important volcanic rocks (lavas and tuffs) and associated intrusions in the geosyncline.

The subsiding geosyncline is usually bordered by regions in which subsidence is either absent or much slower. These stable or relatively stable **shelves** are covered by shallow shelf-seas in which sediments of the same age as those in the geosyncline are much thinner. They are also much better sorted because they have been subjected to the winnowing effects of waves and currents during deposition. Typical shelf-sea sediments are mud-free sandstones and shelly or coral limestones – although shales are also common.

There is also a notable difference between the faunas of the shelf-seas and the geosynclinal sea proper. The shallow shelf-seas form a natural habitat for the great majority of bottom-living marine creatures, whose fossil remains can

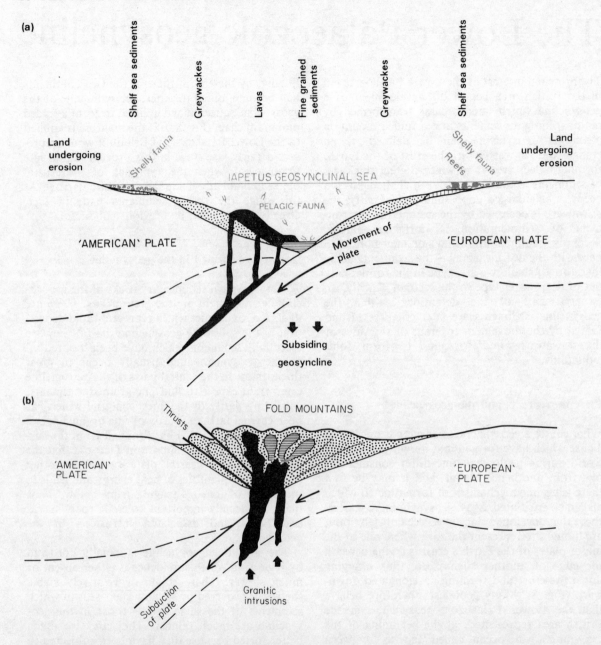

Figure 8 Diagrammatic cross section of an idealised geosyncline

therefore usually be found abundantly in these sediments, forming a 'shelly' faunal facies of such things as brachiopods, lamellibranchs, arthropods and corals. The geosyncline itself is an unfavourable environment for bottom-living animals and the fossil remains in these rocks are usually of **pelagic** (swimming or floating) animals which sank to the bottom only after death. The graptolites

were an example of such creatures in the Lower Palaeozoic.

The above summary is, of course, a very much simplified version of the actual forms of geosynclines, but all the essential features described can be found in the Lower Palaeozoic of Britain.

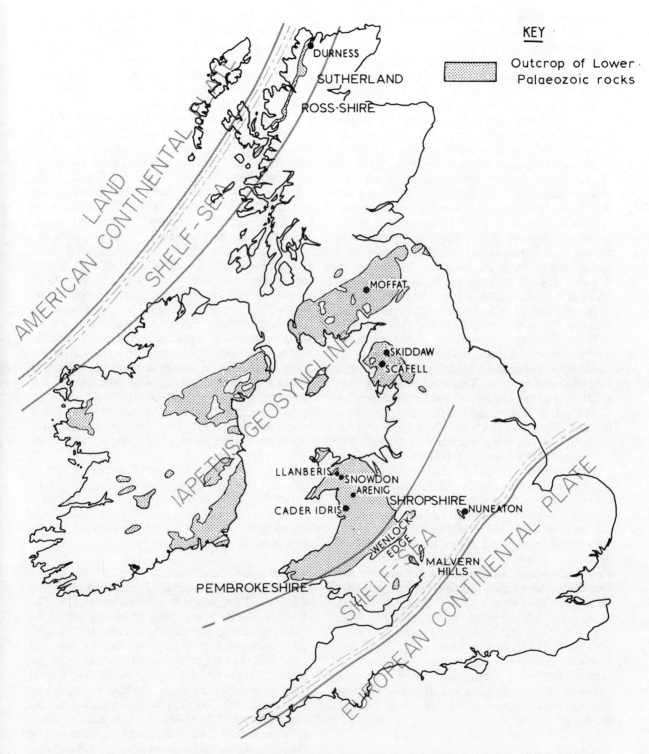

KEY

▨ Outcrop of Lower Palaeozoic rocks

DURNESS

SUTHERLAND

ROSS-SHIRE

MOFFAT

SKIDDAW

SCAFELL

LLANBERIS

SNOWDON

ARENIG

SHROPSHIRE

NUNEATON

CADER IDRIS

WENLOCK EDGE

MALVERN HILLS

PEMBROKESHIRE

LAND

AMERICAN CONTINENTAL PLATE

SHELF-SEA

IAPETUS GEOSYNCLINE

SHELF-SEA

EUROPEAN CONTINENTAL PLATE

Figure 9 Outcrops of Lower Palaeozoic rocks and the geography of Lower Palaeozic times
The distribution of land and sea represents the early Cambrian period – later it was probably more complicated.

The Lower Palaeozoic succession in Britain

The Cambrian

These rocks are seen only here and there as inliers emerging from beneath younger rocks and it is therefore difficult to make out a connected picture. In Wales, where the widest outcrops occur, the Cambrian consists mainly of alternating greywacke-type grits and thick shales. Many of the latter are now in the form of slates, such as the famous Llanberis roofing slates of North Wales. In the Midlands, the Cambrian inliers – notably at Nuneaton, in the Malverns and in Shropshire – show clean-washed quartzites and sandstones at the base followed by thick, unmetamorphosed, shales. Thus, very generally, a geosynclinal facies can be recognised in Wales and a shelf-sea facies in the Midlands – although in this case a predominantly shelly fauna (trilobites and some brachiopods) is found in both.

In northern Scotland, the northwestern outcrops in Sutherland and Ross-shire show a very different Cambrian, essentially of shallow-water sandstones and limestones (the Durness Limestone) with a fauna of trilobites such as *Olenellus* in the Lower Cambrian. This trilobite and its close relatives are characteristic of the North American Cambrian, and are quite different from those found in Wales and England, where *Callavia* is the main Lower Cambrian trilobite and *Paradoxides* the main Middle Cambrian trilobite. (The latter genera are characteristic of Europe but do also occur in extreme eastern North America, where a sharp boundary separates them from *Olenellus* fauna in the Lower Cambrian and another distinctive western group in the Middle Cambrian.) The only linking evidence between these two areas is near the southern edge of the Grampian Highlands where, as mentioned before, the top part of the Dalradian is shown by its rare trilobites to be Cambrian in age. These Upper Dalradian rocks are mainly greywackes of geosynclinal type, thus it is likely that in Cambrian times a northwestern shelf sea, now represented in north-west Scotland and much of North America, was separated from a southeastern shelf sea, now represented in the English Midlands and extreme eastern North America, by the wide oceanic trough of Iapetus.

The Ordovician

This usually lies unconformably on older rocks, Cambrian or Precambrian, indicating that a con-siderable period of folding followed by erosion took place at the end of the Cambrian time. Further important unconformities are found near the top of the Ordovician and beneath the overlying Silurian, each providing evidence of periods of folding, uplift and erosion, probably caused by episodes of plate subduction.

The different facies exhibited by Lower Palaeozoic rocks are well shown in the Ordovician. The geosynclinal facies consists of shales (in places now slates) and greywackes, with a fauna mainly of **graptolites**. The shelf facies consists of sandstones and shales with a **shelly** fauna (brachiopods and trilobites). The third facies is **volcanic**.

All three are well illustrated by the Welsh area. In central Wales thousands of metres of greywackes and mudstones, with widely spaced graptolitic bands, represent rapid accumulation within the geosyncline. The shelf facies seems to have covered only a narrow belt, from Shropshire to Pembrokeshire, and is absent from the Midlands. The volcanic facies is very well developed – hundreds of metres of lavas and tuffs build Snowdon, Cader Idris and the Arenig Mountains. In the Lake District, the lower Ordovician Skiddaw Slates are typical geosynclinal sediments, and are followed upwards by the Borrowdale Volcanic group which forms Helvellyn and Scafell. These volcanic rocks seem to have been piled so high on the floor of the geosyncline that at times they formed dry land.

In the Southern Uplands of Scotland and in Ireland a dominantly geosynclinal facies is again found, but in north-west Scotland the upper part of the Durness Limestone is of Lower Ordovician age so that there must have been shelf-sea conditions there at that time.

The Silurian

The rocks of geosynclinal facies formed during this period are much as in the Ordovician. The Southern Uplands provide a good example of the contrast in the geosyncline at this time between the thick accumulation of greywackes in the marginal parts and the thin pelagic shales further from the source of supply of sediment. Near Moffat, a band of graptolite-bearing shale, 6 metres thick, can be correlated with 300 metres of greywackes a little further north. The Moffat shale is itself overlain by some 1250 metres of greywackes, which can be shown by the contained graptolites to have accumulated in a shorter time than the 6 metres of shale. Thus the belt of rapid deposition had extended outwards and had overwhelmed what was formerly the belt of thin pelagic sediments.

The southeastern shelf sea was well developed in the Silurian; its sandstones, limestones and shales are found not only in the Welsh borderlands but also over a large part of the English Midlands. At times, reef limestones were widspread in the shelf sea – the Wenlock Limestone, which forms Wenlock Edge in Shropshire, is a good example of a fossil reef, with abundant corals and calcareous algae, which must clearly have grown in a very shallow sea. This belt of Silurian reefs can also be traced along the margin of the geosyncline outside the British area, reappearing from beneath younger rocks in Gottland and Estonia and also, as the Niagara Limestone, along the St Lawrence River and in northeastern United States.

In both the Ordovician and the Silurian, graptolites are the most useful fossils for correlating and indicating the age of the sediments, which can be divided into zones characterised by particular species. As most graptolites were pelagic animals, they tended to have a wide geographical distribution and many of the zones recognised in Britain can be used to correlate the rocks over long distances, in some cases even world-wide. In the shallow-water shelf-sea facies, with their shelly fauna, in which graptolites are often rare or absent, brachiopods are stratigraphically useful but, as they are benthonic animals, the distribution of each species is usually more local.

Chapter 4

Map: Fig. 11

The Caledonian mountain-building

The pile of sediments which had accumulated in the Lower Palaeozoic geosyncline was folded and uplifted at the end of the Lower Palaeozoic era to form a range of fold-mountains. This was caused by the impact of the North American and European plates coming together, closing the gap and abolishing the last remnants of the Iapetus Ocean. These movements are named the **Caledonian orogenesis** or **orogeny** – one can hence speak of

Caledonian structures having been imposed on the rocks and of the Caledonian mountains having been produced. As mentioned before, there were several periods of folding of the geosyncline during the course of the Lower Palaeozoic, some of them quite important, which gave rise to unconformities. Some of the unconformities affect only the shelf, or marginal parts, of the geosyncline, since small movements of folding or

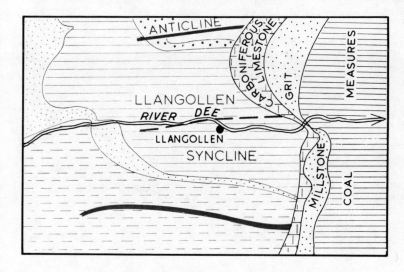

Figure 10 **The Caledonian unconformity**
Sketch-map of part of North Wales, showing how the Upper Palaeozoic rocks lie unconformably upon the Lower Palaeozoic as a result of the Caledonian mountain-building movements.

uplift tend to have little effect upon the deep subsiding basin, while disturbing the normal course of deposition among the shallow seas and thin sediments of the shelf. Thus, in general, the basin tends to be a region of continuous deposition with few breaks while shelf sedimentation tends to be more interrupted by breaks in sedimentation and by unconformities.

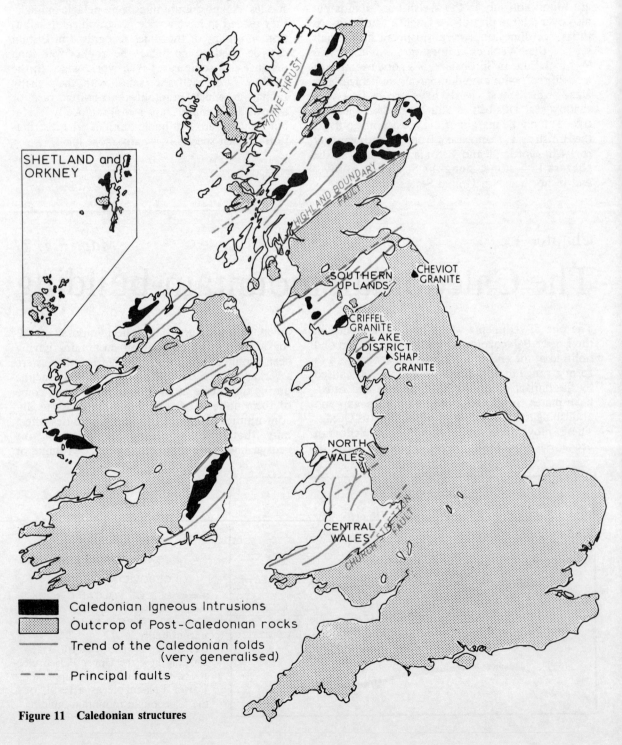

Figure 11 Caledonian structures

Structures formed by the orogeny

The structures produced by the Caledonian orogenesis become less complex from north to south. In the Moinian and Dalradian rocks of the Scottish Highlands folding is intense, usually taking the form of great recumbent folds which have been refolded in a complicated manner. The rocks in this area have also been thoroughly metamorphosed by the effects of the orogenesis. In the Southern Uplands, the Lake District, North Wales and the corresponding parts of Ireland and the Isle of Man, the Lower Palaeozoic rocks are strongly folded, but the folding is less complex than in the Highlands, and they have been metamorphosed only slightly – shales have become slates. In central Wales the folding is simpler still and the rocks hardly metamorphosed at all. There are at least two reasons for these differences:

(a) The Moinian and Dalradian were involved in more than one major period of folding. The Moinian, at least, was probably folded first in the late Precambrian, then the main Caledonian folding period seems to have been much earlier in the Highlands than further south – either mid-Cambrian or mid-Ordovician or both. These rocks would then have been affected to a certain extent again by the end-Silurian folding, which was the main period of movement in the Southern Uplands and further south, all these Lower Palaeozoic movements being phases of the Caledonian orogeny.

(b) Owing to the earlier main folding and to repeated uplift and erosion, the Highlands exhibit a deeper level in the folded mountain structure than the areas further south – a level at which more intense or higher-grade metamorphism had been induced.

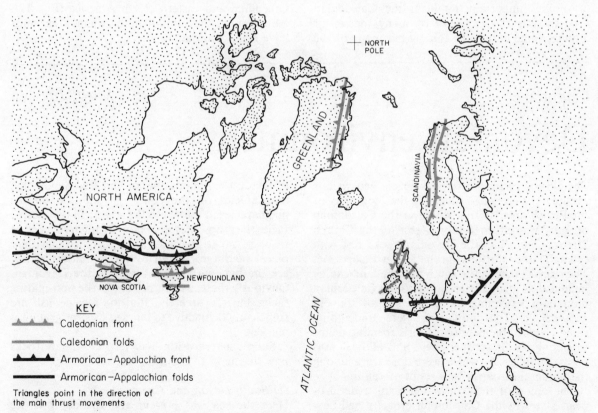

Figure 12 **Simplified map of the present-day distribution of the Caledonian and Armorican–Appalachian fold systems**

The importance of the end-Silurian phase of folding is that it was the culminating phase of the Caledonian orogeny in the sense that it resulted in the permanent abolition of the geosyncline as such, and its replacement by a range of fold mountains. Powerful faults also developed at this time, and those present before were intensified. In north-west Scotland the Moinian rocks were pushed for many miles northwestwards over the unmetamorphosed rocks of the shelf area, along the thrust faults of the Moine Thrust system (see Fig. 6, p. 8). The series of great NE–SW faults so characteristic of Britain's geological structure – such as the Great Glen, Highland Boundary, Southern Upland and Church Stretton Faults – were all strongly re-emphasised. The Church Stretton Fault is especially interesting as it marks the general southeastern limit of the true Caledonian structures – beyond it was the southeastern shelf area, or foreland, where the rocks were only gently folded.

Another important result of the Caledonian orogeny was the intrusion of many masses of granite, some during the folding but many of the best-known ones as a late stage of the process, in early Devonian times. The Criffel granite of southern Scotland, and the Cheviot and Shap granites of northern England are examples of this.

It must be emphasised that the present-day mountains of Scotland, the Lake District and Wales are not in any sense the worn-down stumps of the Caledonian mountains. The latter were long ago eroded away completely and the present mountains, as **topographic** features, are all *young*, dating only from the Tertiary. Only the *structure* of the rocks is inherited from the Caledonian orogeny.

From Figure 11 it can be seen that, generally, the folds produced by the Caledonian orogeny trend SW–NE, as this was the orientation of the junction, or **suture**, between the two crustal plates. Following this trend northeastwards, the same Caledonian folds are found running the length of the Scandinavian peninsula. Even more significantly, these folds are also found in eastern Greenland and eastern North America (Fig. 12). At the end of the Silurian all these land areas must have been continuous.

Chapter 5

Map: Fig. 13

Devonian environments

The closing of the Lower Palaeozoic geosyncline resulted in a complete change in the geography of the British area, so that wherever the Caledonian orogeny was effective (north-west of the Church Stretton fault line) the Devonian rocks rest with dramatic unconformity on the Lower Palaeozoic. The sea was now in the south and the land can be imagined as gradually rising up to the Caledonian mountains extending along the line of the old geosyncline. The mountains were undergoing rapid erosion, the resulting debris forming deltas extending to the southern sea, and alluvial fans poured into basins which were appearing among the mountains, partly as a result of faulting.

The union of the North American and European plates by the Caledonian orogeny had now formed a large continent, the 'Old Red Sandstone Continent', of which the British area was a part (Fig. 14). The Devonian sediments therefore can be divided into two **magnafacies**, or major groups

of facies: the non-marine, or Old Red Sandstone, magnafacies on the continent and the marine magnafacies in the sea to the south. In the marine facies the graptolites were now so much reduced as to be of no stratigraphical importance and their place was largely taken by the **goniatites**, which are the best correlation fossils in the Devonian. Obviously these are not present in the non-marine facies but, fortunately, the non-marine **fish** are sufficiently distinctive to be used as stratigraphical markers.

Subsequent erosion has left Devonian rocks now visible in five chief areas.

(1) South Devon and Cornwall
Here the sea was present and the deposits are almost entirely marine, of distinctly shallow-water type at first with sandstones and, notably, reef limestones with corals, as seen at Torquay and Plymouth. The Upper Devonian, however, is

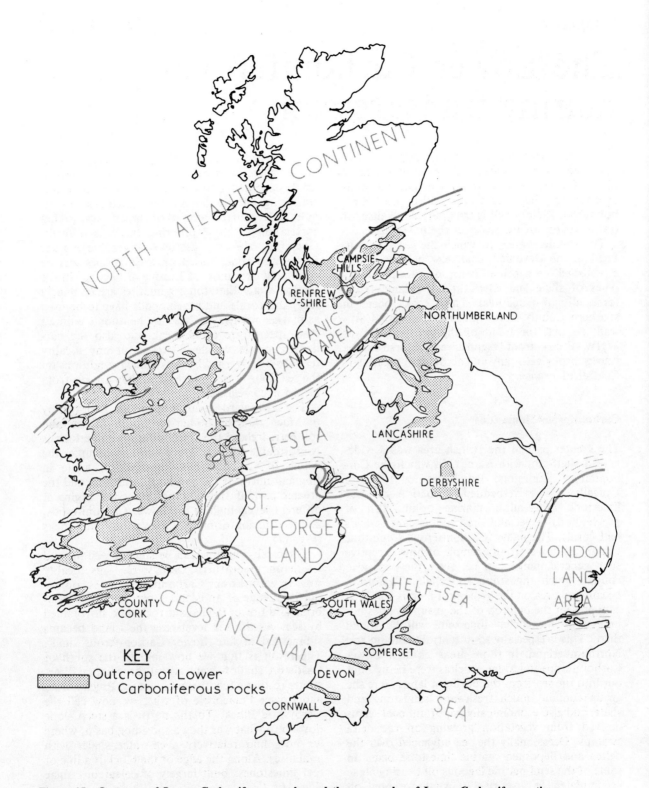

Figure 15 Outcrops of Lower Carboniferous rocks and the geography of Lower Carboniferous times
The geography represents a time late in the Lower Carboniferous when the sea had spread from the south over a large part of the British area.

The Lower Carboniferous marine transgression

By this time the old Caledonian mountains were much reduced by erosion, and the essential feature of the Lower Carboniferous, which corresponds broadly to the rock-group called the 'Carboniferous Limestone', is the gradual advance, or transgression, of the sea over the lower areas.

The southern area, to which the sea was confined in the Devonian, had now become a well established geosyncline, with deep-water rock-types of shale and chert, and a pelagic fauna (especially of goniatites). These rocks occur in southern County Cork and in Devon and Cornwall, so that the trend of the geosyncline was WNW–ESE – from Devonshire its course can be traced through Brittany and across into the Massif Central of France.

Carboniferous 'Limestone'

The greater part of the British area was a widespread shelf-sea, with islands, in which the Carboniferous Limestone was deposited. This is typically a massive-bedded formation of grey limestone of shallow marine origin, full of brachiopods (especially the productids), crinoids and corals. The name 'Carboniferous Limestone Group' is, however, an example of how deceptive such general names can be, since the beds also contain much sandstone and shale. Therefore, because an area on the geological map is coloured to represent the outcrop of the group, it does not necessarily mean that limestone will be found there. This is especially so in central Scotland and Northumberland. In those areas, in later Lower Carboniferous times, large deltas were being built out into the sea from the northern land. Here the group contains much freshwater sandstone and shale, and also economically important coal seams derived from vegetation growing on the delta swamps. Occasionally the sea advanced over the deltas and deposited marine limestone beds. In some of the semi-marine lagoons oil-bearing algae accumulated to give rise to what are now oil shales.

In deeper subsiding basins within the shelf-sea, marine shales were deposited – as seen in parts of Derbyshire and Lancashire. The fauna of these, consisting of goniatites and lamellibranchs, is quite different from that of the limestones, so that correlation of these differing facies is difficult. Goniatites are very useful stratigraphic marker fossils and zones based on their species can be correlated over most of Europe or beyond. In the shallow-water limestones goniatites are extremely rare, and corals and brachiopods have to be used as marker fossils. As these are benthonic animals their species are often local, and also the particular species which is present at any locality tends to be governed by the detailed conditions on the sea floor at that place, thus they are far from ideal for correlation.

The northward advance of the sea is shown by the fact that in Somerset, South Wales and southern Ireland the Carboniferous Limestone is conformable with the Devonian and occupies the whole of the Lower Carboniferous, while in England north of the southern Midlands, and the greater part of Ireland, the succession begins at different levels high in the Lower Carboniferous, and rests unconformably upon various older rocks (Fig. 17).

These relationships can be studied well around Castleton in northern Derbyshire. This locality was, in early Lower Carboniferous times, on the northern edge of an island composed of Precambrian and Lower Palaeozoic rocks and surrounded by sea. As the sea level rose the island became submerged in late Lower Carboniferous times. The result is that we now find to the south of Castleton shallow-water coral–brachiopod limestones resting unconformably on the Precambrian and Lower Palaeozoic of what we now call the Derbyshire Block. To the north is a steep slope down into what was then a subsiding basin, where we now find relatively deep-water shales with goniatites. Along the edge of the block is a line of reef limestones, built largely of calcareous algae (Fig. 16).

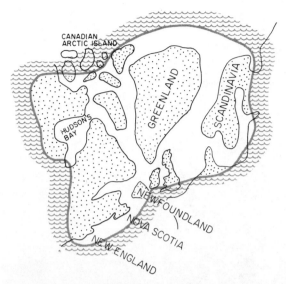

Figure 14 The Old Red Sandstone continent
Present land areas are shown in approximately the relative positions they would have occupied in Devonian times. The area of sea is shown at its maximum; during parts of the Devonian there was more land and less sea.

largely of deep-water shales with a pelagic fauna – these give evidence of the formation of a new geosyncline, as will be seen in subsequent chapters. The shallow-water shelly fauna is much like that of the Silurian – dominated by brachiopods and corals – but the goniatites were now the most important fossils of the pelagic fauna in deeper marine conditions. Most of the shales are now in the form of slates.

(2) North Devon and West Somerset (Exmoor and the Quantocks)
The main interest here is that marine shales and limestones alternate with non-marine red sandstones containing plant remains. Thus the margin of the sea was fluctuating across this area during the whole Devonian period.

(3) South Wales, the Welsh Borderland and Southern Ireland
Here the sediments are almost entirely of non-marine (semi-marine to freshwater) origin and the environment can be thought of as a series of deltas sloping down from the Caledonian mountains to the sea. The Old Red Sandstone rocks consist mainly of red sandstones, seen well in the Brecon Beacons and the Black Mountains, and red mudstones, wrongly called 'marls' (a marl contains calcium carbonate, these rocks usually do not). The fossils are mainly of plants and fish, and this is particularly interesting because, although both were in existence in Lower Palaeozoic times,

it is not until the Old Red Sandstone that they are found in large numbers or well preserved. In Breconshire, Pembrokeshire and County Cork there are a few marine beds in the upper Old Red Sandstone, showing that the sea did at times reach as far north as this.

(4) Central Scotland (including the Cheviot and Oban areas and Northern Ireland)
Here, there is no sign of marine deposits in the Old Red Sandstone. The great thicknesses of breccias, conglomerates and red sandstones suggest that the environment was an arid intermontane basin, like some of the Central Asian basins of today. The basin must also have contained many volcanoes, perhaps connected with the faulting movements that were going on, as the rocks contain some 1900 metres of lavas and tuffs which form the Cheviot, Pentland, Ochil and Sidlaw Hills.

(5) Northern Scotland (including Orkney and Shetland)
Here again the beds are non-marine and the lowest and highest parts of the Old Red Sandstone are in general like those of central Scotland. The main part, however, consists of some 4000 metres of thin-bedded sandstones and mudstones, with some limestones, called the Caithness Flags. Again fish are the main fossils and these beds were certainly deposited in a body of non-marine water, probably a large lake.

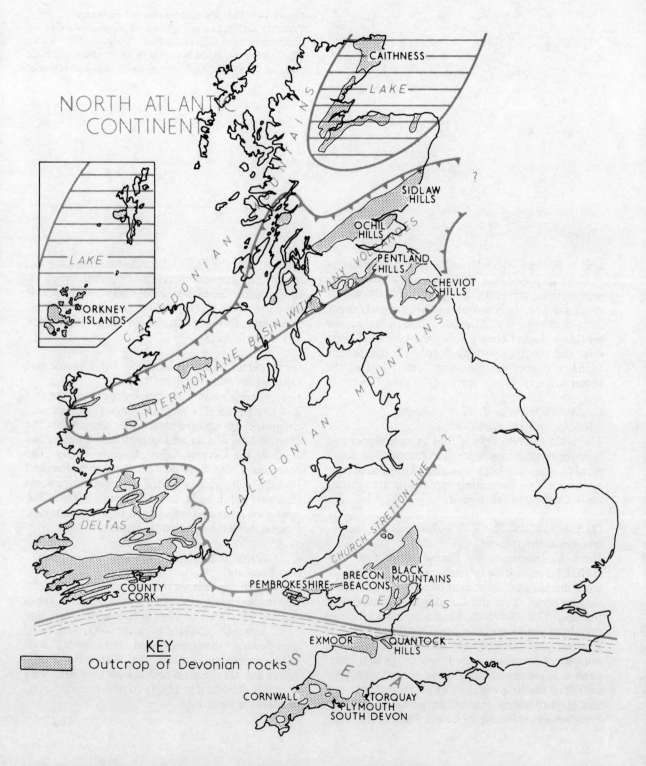

Figure 13 Outcrops of Devonian rocks and the geography of Devonian times

Figure 16 Marine environments in north Derbyshire in late Lower Carboniferous times

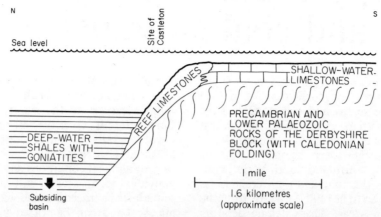

Figure 17 Combs Quarry, Foredale, North Yorkshire
The horizontal Lower Carboniferous limestone above is resting with obvious unconformity upon the Silurian beds below, which dip southwards (to the left).

Lower Carboniferous volcanic activity

Another difference which the central Scottish Lower Carboniferous shows is the great importance of volcanic activity. There were great outpourings of lava among the deltas, especially of basalt, much of which builds the Clyde basalt plateau of Renfrewshire and the Campsie Hills. Many of the actual sites of the volcanoes are known. Volcanic rocks also occur among the English and Irish Carboniferous Limestone, but on a smaller scale.

The Upper Carboniferous deltas and coal swamps

In southern Scotland and in England as far south as north Yorkshire, the formation of deltaic deposits with coal seams and occasional marine limestones, and with lavas (described in the last chapter) continued uninterruptedly into the Upper Carboniferous. Further south, as now seen in the southern Pennines, North and South Wales, conditions changed at this time and a different series of great deltas began to be built outwards from the neighbouring land areas. These deltaic deposits form the **Millstone Grit**, the most characteristic rock-type of which is thick coarse sandstone, or 'grit', representing deltaic sandbanks. These grits are best seen on the south Pennine moors, especially in the Peak District. The change in lithology must reflect uplift of the land areas and increased transport of eroded, land-derived detritus into the sea.

Away from the influence of the deltas, as in western Ireland, the sea was not clear and shallow, as it had been in Carboniferous Limestone times, but was muddy. Hence the characteristic marine deposits were shales, with a fauna mainly of goniatites. From time to time the sea, with this type of sedimentation, spread over the deltas so that the non-marine deltaic deposits are interrupted by **shale marine bands**, which are very useful for correlation. Here also, at times when the delta surfaces were above sea level, vegetation flourished and gave rise to coal seams, although in the Millstone Grit they are not thick enough to be economically workable.

The Coal Measures

By later Upper Carboniferous times, when the Coal Measures were deposited, most of Britain (and some of northern Europe) had been levelled by erosion. Uplands remained in the north (Scottish Highlands) and the centre (central Wales and the southern Midlands). In the south there was still the geosyncline, filled with a great thickness of greywackes in the Upper Carboniferous, but occasionally emerging above sea level, when non-

marine beds with poor coals were formed. These poor coals are called 'culm' and give the name Culm Measures to the whole of the Devonshire Carboniferous. Over the rest of the country there were generally deltaic conditions like those of Millstone Grit times. There was great uniformity of geographical conditions shown by the fact that individual coal seams and marine bands can sometimes be traced far and wide – one individual marine band can be traced in all the coalfields from Ireland to southern Russia. Northern Europe must have been a vast level deltaic swamp, much of it covered in dense forest.

In these conditions the typical Coal Measures were formed. These beds are characterised by a rhythmic type of sedimentation (Fig. 19). It is normally found that a coal seam, representing a growth of dense swamp forest, is overlain by shales with marine fossils, showing that the sea had flooded over the delta flats. These pass up into more shales, but with a fauna of non-marine lamellibranchs: the sea had retreated and given place to brackish or freshwater lagoonal conditions. The shales became sandy upwards and pass up into a thick sandstone member, with scattered plant remains, which evidently represents river-borne sandbanks, suggesting that the higher land bordering the delta flats had been uplifted leading to more rapid erosion. As the impetus of this uplift died away the sand became finer and eventually swamp forest again spread over the delta, giving rise to another coal seam. Usually beneath the coal seam is a bed called the **seat-earth** which may be either clay, then called 'fire-clay', or sandstone, then called 'ganister'. This bed is the soil in which the coal plants grew and their roots are characteristically found in it. Seat-earth has had many of the fluxing materials, such as alkalis, removed by the plants and is therefore relatively infusible. This makes it valuable for manufacture of fire-bricks and furnace linings.

The plants found in the Coal Measures are valuable both for correlation purposes and for the information which they give about the conditions of the time. The British Coal Measures, together

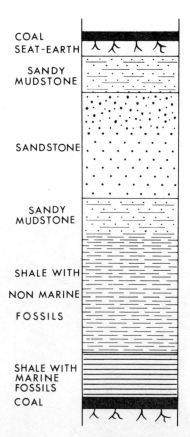

COAL
SEAT-EARTH

SANDY
MUDSTONE

SANDSTONE

SANDY
MUDSTONE

SHALE WITH
NON MARINE
FOSSILS

SHALE WITH
MARINE
FOSSILS
COAL

Figure 19 A Coal Measure cyclothem
The diagram represents an ideal cyclothem. In fact one
or other element in the rhythmic sequence is frequently
found to be missing.

with those of central Europe through to southern
Russia and of the eastern United States, have a
particularly rich flora. This agrees with other lines
of evidence that Britain at that time lay further
south in the tropical zone of the Earth.

Cyclic sedimentation
The rhythmic unit of sedimentation described
above is called a **cyclothem** (Fig. 19) and the Coal
Measures are essentially composed of such
cyclothems scores of times repeated. Note that
only a very small part of the Coal Measures is
actually coal; and even so the plant debris was in
some cases removed by erosion before the overlying shale was deposited, so that the same rhythms
of sedimentation may be found but with practic-
ally no coal seams at all. This is the case with
much of the widespread Coal Measures of Ireland
and the uppermost parts of the Coal Measures of
England and Wales. Likewise, in many
cyclothems the marine episode is missing.

The cyclothemic type of sedimentation, which
occurs not only in the Coal Measures but also in
the typical Millstone Grit and in the northern
deltaic facies (**Yoredale** facies) of the Lower Carboniferous, gives rise to a characteristic type of
scenery because of the more or less regular alter-
nations of sandstones and shales, with limestones
in addition in the Yoredale facies. The sandstones
and limestones are resistant to weathering and
stand out as ledges while the shales weather to
gentle slopes. This gives a stepped topography
seen, for example, on the slopes of Ingle-
borough (Yoredale facies) (Fig. 20), in the Millstone Grit
valleys of the southern Pennines between Man-
chester, Huddersfield and Sheffield, or in the Coal
Measure valleys of the South Wales coalfield.

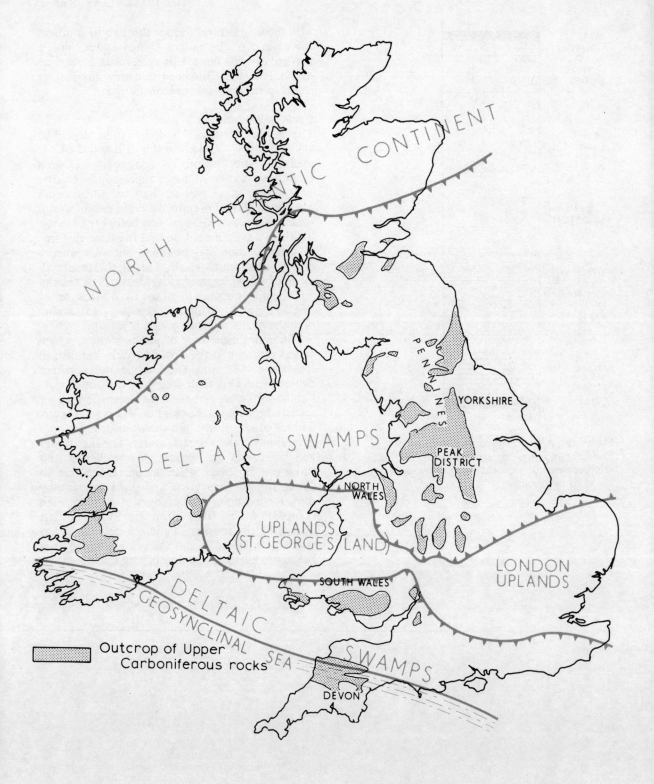

Figure 18   Outcrops of Upper Carboniferous rocks and the geography of Upper Carboniferous times

Figure 20   Twistleton Scars, near Ingleton, Yorkshire
On the valley sides the stepped topography is caused by the outcrop of limestone bands in the Lower Carboniferous. In the background above the limestone (light-coloured), the mountain of Whernside is composed of the Yoredale beds (darker-coloured) with a prominent sandstone band forming a step in the profile. The summit of Whernside is capped by the Millstone Grit.

The Armorican mountain-building

As mentioned in the last chapter, the highest parts of the Coal Measures in most of the British coalfields are barren of coal. The beds here are usually red sandstones and red shales, with some conglomerates, hence the miners' term 'Barren Red Beds' for these horizons. In the Midland coalfields these pass up into really coarse conglomerates and breccias. Another important point is that marine bands cease to occur about halfway up the Coal Measures. All these facts point to increasing uplift of the British area, with uplands which had been subject to tropical weathering (to give the red colouring) and were undergoing increasingly rapid erosion. The next beds that can be dated are of Upper Permian age and rest with violent unconformity on the Carboniferous.

All these phenomena are due to the occurrence of another major period of mountain-building, the **Armorican** (or **Hercynian**) orogeny, similar in scale to the Caledonian. These folding movements began in the south of Europe well back in Carboniferous times, but the main phase reached southern Britain towards the end of the Upper Carboniferous. The southern geosyncline was obliterated and transformed into a folded mountain chain stretching across what is now southern Ireland, southern England and Brittany. The Devonian and Carboniferous sediments in Devon and Cornwall show complex structures, including intense isoclinal folding (well seen on the coast near Bude) and major northward thrusting. Most of the shales have been metamorphosed to slate. The shelf-sea rocks on the margin show similar, but less intense, structures, as in the anticlines of the Mendip Hills and of the south coast of Wales, especially in Pembrokeshire. These structures plunge eastwards beneath the younger rocks of south-east England, where they are undoubtedly present at depth.

The general effect was to produce folding along approximately east–west trends in the area of the Upper Palaeozoic geosyncline and its immediate northern margins (Fig. 21). Further north, this period of tectonic movement produced broader,

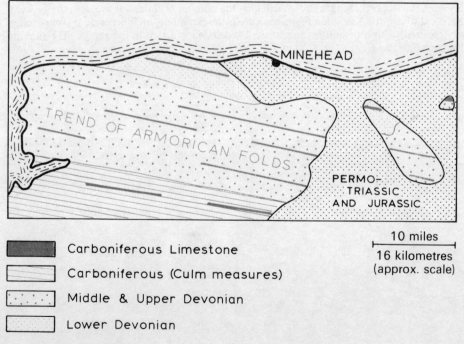

Figure 21   The Armorican unconformity
Sketch-map of part of north Devon and Somerset, showing how the Mesozoic rocks lie unconformably upon the Upper Palaeozoic as a result of the Armorican mountain-building movements.

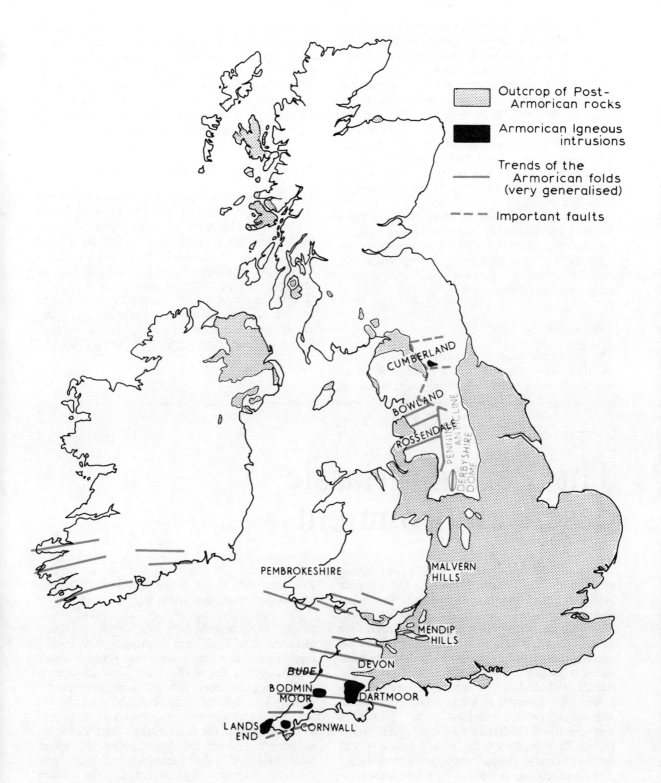

Figure 22 Armorican structures

Legend:

- Outcrop of Post-Armorican rocks
- Armorican Igneous intrusions
- Trends of the Armorican folds (very generalised)
- Important faults

Map labels:

CUMBERLAND
BOWLAND
ROSSENDALE
PENNINE ANTICLINE
DERBYSHIRE DOME
PEMBROKESHIRE
MALVERN HILLS
MENDIP HILLS
BUDE
DEVON
BODMIN MOOR
DARTMOOR
LANDS END
CORNWALL

more open folds, some approximately east–west or NE–SW (like the Rossendale and Bowland folds of Lancashire) but also some important ones with a north–south trend. Examples of these are the Pennine Anticline, between Lancashire and Yorkshire, and the associated Derbyshire Dome; and the Malvern Hills with their associated north–south folds. There is clear evidence that some of the north–south folds, at least those of the Malvern area, were formed about halfway through Coal Measure times as an early folding phase, before the main phase with its east–west folds had begun.

One important result of these two directions taken by the Armorican folds is the breaking up of the uniform sheet of Coal Measures into the separate coalfields seen today, all of which are, broadly speaking, down-warped syncline-type Armorican structures.

Igneous activity

The Armorican orogeny, like the Caledonian, was closely followed by the intrusion among the folded sediments of granites – those of Dartmoor, Bodmin Moor and the other granites of Cornwall down to Lands End and the Scilly Isles. Associated with the granites was an important phase of mineralisation, when the tin and copper deposits of Cornwall and Devon were formed. Most of the lead and zinc veins found in the Carboniferous Limestone (as in the Mendips, Derbyshire and Cumberland) also date from this period.

Armorican plate movements

The Armorican orogeny was caused in broad terms by the collision of the northern, Euro-North American crustal plate, which had been formed in the Caledonian orogeny, with a southern crustal plate which we could call African – South American, although in detail the Armorican orogeny is more complicated than that – more complex in fact than the Caledonian orogeny. The result is that the Armorican folds can be traced across central Europe and also, like the Caledonian folds, into eastern North America (Fig. 12).

Chapter 9

Map: Fig. 23

The Permo-Triassic desert environment

It is usually difficult to separate clearly the Permian system from the Triassic in Britain. The Permian is regarded as the last period of the Upper Palaeozoic era, and the Triassic as the first of the Mesozoic era, because of a considerable difference in the fossil faunas seen where these periods are represented by fully marine strata. The Permian fauna is broadly reminiscent of the Carboniferous, but the Triassic fauna is in many respects a fore-taste of the Jurassic. In Britain both periods are, almost everywhere, represented by non-marine and poorly fossiliferous deposits. Even where marine Permian does occur it has a restricted and not very typical fauna. Hence both periods are often lumped together as the **New Red Sandstone** – the group of dominantly non-marine strata coming above the Carboniferous just as the Old Red Sandstone is the group of dominantly non-marine strata coming below it.

This treatment emphasises the similarity between the Old and the New Red Sandstone groups of formations. Both were formed, broadly speaking, in periods when Britain was predominantly land following the uplift which resulted from a major orogeny. Both rest with dramatic uncomformity on the older rocks folded by the orogeny. Both represent a completely new set of geographical conditions in the British area. The Caledonian orogeny had joined the American and European plates into an Old Red Sandstone continent. Now the Armorican orogeny had joined on the African – South American plate and, about the same

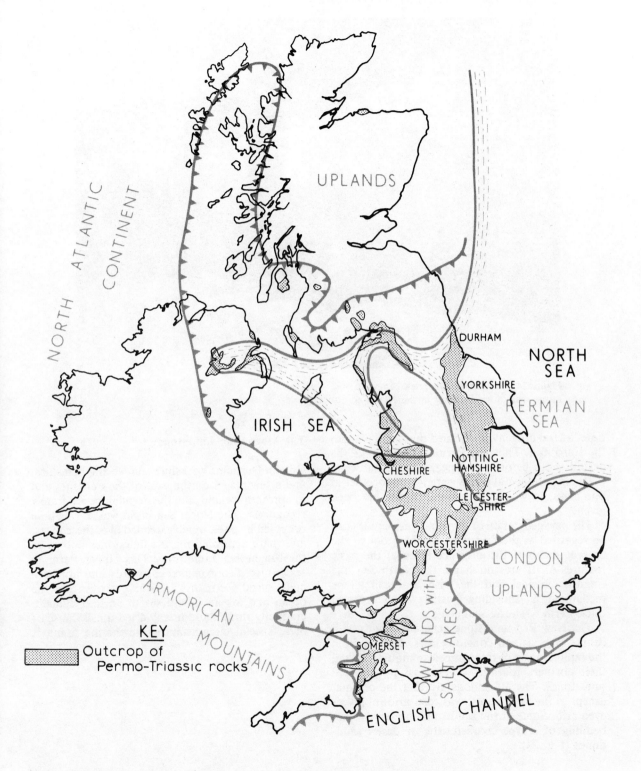

Figure 23 Outcrops of Permo-Triassic rocks and the geography of Permo-Triassic times
The sea was in the position shown only during the later part of the Permian period.

Figure 24   Mauchline Quarries, Ayrshire
Large-scale dune bedding in the New Red Sandstone.

time, a Ural orogeny had joined the Asian plate to the European. Thus the Permo-Trias, unlike the periods both before and since, was a time when the main continental plates were joined together in one mass, to which the name **Pangaea** has been given.

The new geography of Permo-Triassic times can be regarded as the first faint blocking out of the present shape of Britain since three of the basic features of its present shape, the North Sea, the English Channel and the Irish Sea, can all be recognised as subsiding basins which received thick Permo-Triassic sediments.

The New Red Sandstone generally begins with coarse breccias and conglomerates, derived from the rapid erosion of the Armorican mountains and their northern foothills. These pass up into red sandstones. The indications are that the climate, except in favoured spots, was semi-arid, in places even arid. Some of the sandstones preserve cross-bedding of a type characteristic of desert sand-dunes (Fig. 24).

The Magnesian Limestone

Only in Durham, Yorkshire and Nottinghamshire, and a few places on the west of the Pennines and in northern Ireland, can the Permian be separately recognised. The North Sea Basin was at this time occupied by a sea which extended over these parts, and there deposited marine limestones known as the **Magnesian Limestone**. This Upper Permian sea (which also extended eastwards into northern and central Germany) became cut off from the ocean and, as an inland sea in an arid climate, gradually shrank and finally dried up. Because of these special circumstances the marine fauna is limited, and dies out upwards in the succession. The drying up of the sea led to the laying down of a series of **evaporite** deposits – salts which came out of solution as the water evaporated. Thus the limestone itself is impregnated with dolomite and is followed upwards by a series of rhythmic deposits of gypsum, rock salt and potassium salts. Some of these are of great economic value both in England and Germany. The Permian sandstone beds of the North Sea Basin are major reservoir rocks for natural gas.

Since the climate was generally dry throughout Permo-Triassic times, evaporite deposits occur at several horizons, especially in the upper beds of the New Red Sandstone, which are undoubtedly Triassic in age. Gypsum occurs in many places, especially in Nottinghamshire and Leicestershire, where it has been quarried for centuries. Rock salt occurs in commercially workable quantities in Lancashire, Cheshire, Worcestershire and Somerset.

The Mercia Mudstone

The highest beds of the Triassic are of red mudstone formerly called the Keuper Marl (a misnomer, as with the Old Red Sandstone 'marls')
but now known as the **Mercia Mudstone**. This formation is remarkable for its uniformity, as it is much the same wherever it occurs, throughout western Europe. Its uniformity marks the virtual peneplanation of the Armorican mountains. All the lower-lying areas by this time were reduced to a monotonous semi-arid plain covered by red dust – mainly the wind-borne product of tropical weathering in the more upland areas – which now forms the Mercia Mudstone. Important salt deposits in the Mercia Mudstone show that at times salt lakes must have diversified the surface of the plain.

One of the best places to study the Permo-Trias is in south-east Devonshire, where the whole sequence can be seen. At the base, near Torquay and Teignmouth, are the basal breccias and conglomerates, resting with dramatic unconformity on Upper Palaeozoic rocks and full of fragments of Devonian limestone. Eastwards along the coast are sandstones, which show dune bedding very well north of Dawlish, and the Mercia Mudstone succeeds around Sidmouth.

Chapter 10

Map: Fig. 25

The fluctuating shelf-seas of the Jurassic

The Armorican orogeny abolished the last geosyncline in the British area. After it the nearest geosynclinal sea was on the site of what is now the Mediterranean and the Alps – a sea to which geologists have given the name **Tethys**. This was bordered, in the usual way, by shelf-seas whose constantly-changing shapes occupied central and northern Europe during the Mesozoic.

The Rhaetic

The northern shelf-sea of Tethys first advanced over the British area at the very end of the Triassic, laying down the **Rhaetic Beds**, which, although technically Triassic, are dealt with here because they mark the beginning of typically Jurassic conditions. The sea advanced slowly, but very uniformly, over the flat plain of Mercia Mudstone. The Rhaetic Beds, therefore, are much the same throughout western Europe – except where they take the form of beach deposits against those upland masses that were still present, such as the Mendip Hills. Generally, they are black shales and fine-grained limestone, representing semi-marine or 'not-quite-fully-marine' lagoonal conditions.

The Lias and the first British ammonites

As the sea continued to advance, fully marine con-ditions came in. With them appeared the first **ammonites** in the British succession, to the great benefit of the stratigrapher, as ammonites are the most useful of all groups of fossils as strati-graphical markers. This is because, firstly, the ammonites evolved rapidly into new genera and species. Secondly, as free-swimming animals they were geographically widespread. Thirdly, because of the large amount of detail on the shells of most ammonites, evolutionary changes can be easily seen and the different species easily recognised. Thus both the Jurassic and the Cretaceous have been divided up into a large number of ammonite **zones** which can be used for correlation over wide intercontinental areas.

These fully marine beds are the Lower Jurassic or **Lias**. They also are very uniform, especially at first, consisting generally of rapidly alternating shale and limestone at the bottom (Fig. 26), pass-ing up into sands and then shales at the top, with local sands. Fossils are usually abundant, as well as ammonites, belemnites are common and, in the Middle Lias, brachiopods. Many skeletons of the great sea reptiles, the ichthyosaurs and plesiosaurs, have been found. A point of great economic im-portance is the local occurrence of **iron ores**. These are sedimentary oolitic ironstones, con-sisting essentially of **ooliths** (small spherical rock particles with concentrially banded interiors) of iron silicate in a matrix of iron carbonate. They occur especially in the Middle Lias around Ban-bury, Oxfordshire; in the Cleveland Hills of north-east Yorkshire; and also in the Lower Lias

of north Lincolnshire, where they were the basis for foundation of the Scunthorpe steel industry.

The Middle Jurassic

In contrast to the uniformity of at least the lower part of the Lias, the Middle Jurassic rocks which come above are extremely varied. The general pic-ture is that uplift of the land was taking place at the beginning of and during Middle Jurassic time, so that the area became one of very shallow seas with many islands. There were very varying types of sedimentation and a generally shelly fauna of brachiopods, echinoids and corals, into which non-marine deltaic deposits were being built from the lands.

The Middle Jurassic is divided into two main formations, the **Inferior Oolite** below and the **Great Oolite** above, but these formation names, like that of the Carboniferous Limestone, cover a multitude of rock types. In the Cotswold Hills both formations are indeed mainly of thick, cross-bedded oolitic limestone – some of it famous as building stone, such as the Bath Stone (Great Oolite) – with also some coral-reef limestone. So, the sea there was not only shallow but clear and warm, with currents piling up the calcareous ooliths into cross-bedded banks. South of Bath the Great Oolite contains more clay than limestones alternate with non-marine (deltaic) clays and sands, but at the base of the Inferior Oolite there is a very important horizon of iron ore, similar to that of the Lias, which is worked around Kettering and Wellingborough – this is the Northamptonshire Sand Ironstone.

In Yorkshire, the Middle Jurassic has a com-pletely different aspect. Here part of a large delta is preserved and the rocks consist mainly of massive sandstones with thin coal seams, very reminiscent of the Millstone Grit. These beds are famous for their well preserved plant remains. This deltaic facies is also found in the Hebrides and in north-east Scotland, at least in the Great Oolite. The presence of a north British landmass, undergoing erosion can therefore be inferred.

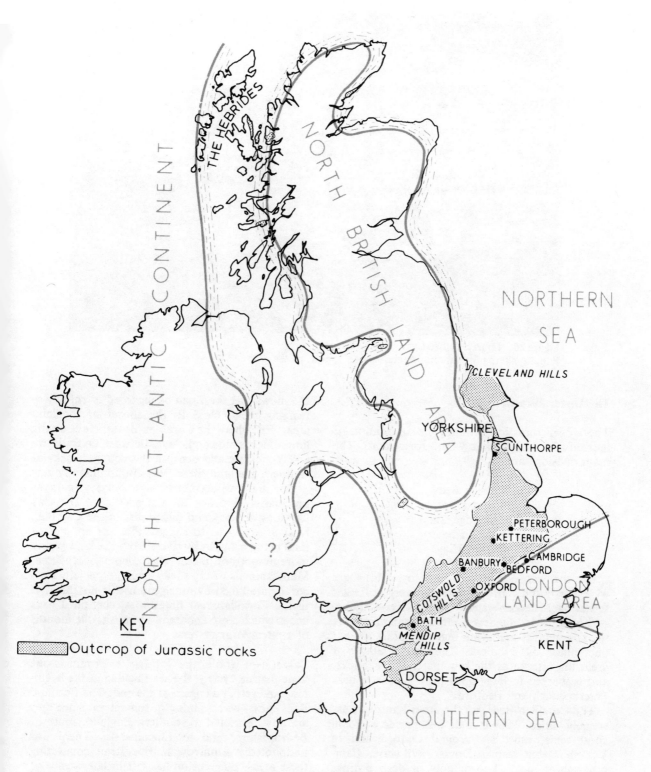

Figure 25 Outcrops of Jurassic rocks and the geography of Jurassic times

Figure 26 Church Cliffs, Lyme Regis, Dorset
Rapidly alternating limestones and shales, typical of the Lower Lias.

The Upper Jurassic

The Upper Jurassic continues the alternation of more uniform with more varied formations. The main divisions are:

Purbeck Beds
Portland Beds
Kimmeridge Clay
Corallian Beds
Oxford Clay

On the whole, the two clay formations are widespread and uniform and probably represent somewhat deeper-water marine conditions. Although their faunas are mixed, ammonites are the dominant element, but marine reptiles are not uncommon, as in the Lias. The Oxford Clay is of great importance as the raw material for bricks, and is worked in large open pits, especially near Peterborough and Bedford.

The Corallian Beds, on the other hand, are extremely varied. They include well preserved fossil coral reefs, especially around Oxford and in Yorkshire, but also in Dorset, Wiltshire, Cambridgeshire and – known only in deep borings beneath the younger rocks – Kent. The map (Fig. 25) shows that these can be regarded essentially as fringing reefs, close to the shores of the land areas. Elsewhere the Corallian Beds include oolitic limestones, sands and clays. Between Oxfordshire and Yorkshire and beneath the younger rocks of southern England these beds are dominantly clay – this is a warning not to take a clayey facies as necessarily evidence of a deeper sea. The clay lithology appears and disappears in the Corallian in such a way as to suggest that the amount of mud being brought by rivers from the lands was a more important factor than depth of the sea. Many animals of the shelly fauna, especially reef-corals, are killed by much mud. It is notable that in the Corallian reef limestones, clay-filled gaps occur which were apparently opposite the mouths of contemporary rivers.

Taken as a whole, the Jurassic in Britain is one huge marine cycle – the sea invaded at the beginning and retreated again at the end. The Portland Beds show the beginning of this retreat since they are now restricted to southern England, south of Bedfordshire, and to Lincolnshire. There was undoubtedly a narrow marine strait connecting these areas, but erosion has left little evidence of it. The Portland Beds in the south consist of sands and limestones, including the famous Portland building stone of Dorset. This is a fine-grained oolitic limestone with a shelly marine fauna, including many large ammonites.

The Purbeck Beds show the maximum retreat of the sea. They are confined to the same areas as the Portland Beds. In the south they are almost entirely non-marine, consisting of freshwater lagoonal limestones and marls, with such freshwater molluscs as *Viviparus* and *Unio*, and also fossil

soils ('dirt-beds') with trees in the position of growth. One or two marine bands occur, but they are without ammonites. The fauna includes terrestrial mammals and insects. This non-marine facies was then widespread in western Europe, but shallow open sea was still present in the North Sea Basin as shown by the equivalent beds in Lincolnshire being sandstones with belemnites and ammonites.

Chapter 11

Map: Fig. 27

The Cretaceous marine transgression

The maximum retreat of the sea demonstrated by the Purbeck Beds also marks the passage from Jurassic to Cretaceous. The base of the Cretaceous, strictly speaking, falls in the middle of the Purbeck Beds, as shown by the zonal ammonites in those areas where they occur at this horizon. In the south of England, south of the London landmass, the freshwater lagoonal or lacustrine deposits of the Upper Purbeck pass up into clearly freshwater sands and clays called the **Wealden Beds** – so called because they outcrop most widely in the Weald. These were formed as the floodplain deposits of rivers coming down from the London 'uplands'. The sea at this time was well away to the south-east, in Tethys, and the south-west in the new Atlantic Sea. The water level rose from time to time over the sand-banks and laid down the clays, and this period ended with a prolonged lacustrine phase, since approximately the top two-thirds of the Wealden Beds consists of the thick **Weald Clay**.

In northern England this lowest part of the Cretaceous is of quite different facies, entirely marine, consisting of clays in Yorkshire, and mainly of sandstones, ironstones and limestones in Lincolnshire. The ammonites and belemnites in these northern outcrops demonstrate that the rocks were laid down in an expanded North Sea basin connected with north Germany and Russia, but not with the seas of south Europe. This shows

that even ammonites are not perfect for correlating strata all over the world since at this time there were two separate **faunal provinces**, a nothern or **boreal** one and a southern or **Tethyan** one, with quite different ammonites and other fossils. Because of this there is still controversy about exactly how the beds are to be correlated between north and south.

The Lower Greensand

In the south, salt water was clearly creeping in during later Wealden times since, although the Weald Clay contains limestone bands with the typical freshwater lake molluscs, its higher part includes horizons with oysters and other animals which do not occur in fresh water. When the main marine transgression came, however, it came abruptly, and rapidly submerged almost the whole of the Wealden mud flats beneath a shallow sea in which the **Lower Greensand** was deposited leaving the London uplands as a land area. The Lower Greensand shows all the variability typical of shallow marine sedimentation. It consists mainly of sandstones, called 'greensands' because of the abundance of the green mineral glauconite, but also of clays and sandy limestones, such as the 'Kentish Rag' of Kent.

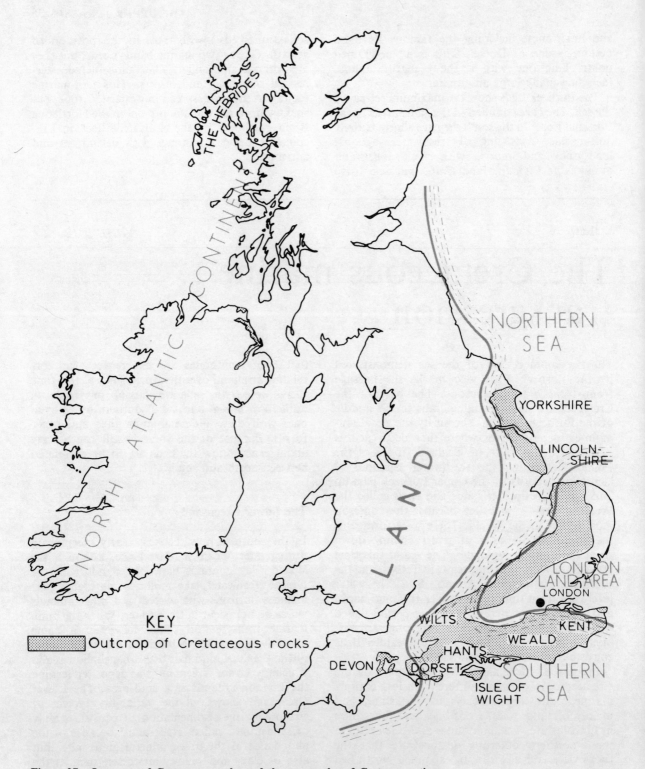

Figure 27 Outcrops of Cretaceous rocks and the geography of Cretaceous times
The distribution of land and sea represents the time when the Lower Greensand was being deposited. Before this the sea was more restricted, while in the Upper Cretaceous it was much more widespread.

The Gault Clay and Upper Greensand

After this, the history of the Cretaceous period was essentially that of an almost continuous marine transgression. In the latter part of Lower Greensand times, the sea over southern England joined up on the one hand with that over northern England and the North Sea, and on the other with that over central and southern France (Fig. 27 illustrates this). The next phase was the submergence of the London land area, since the **Gault Clay**, which conformably overlies the Lower Greensand in the Weald and the Isle of Wight, is found in all the borings put down in the London area, where it rests unconformably on the Palaeozoic rocks of the old London landmass. The beds of Gault Clay age provide a good example of lateral change of facies: in east Kent there is nothing but Gault Clay between the Lower Greensand and the Chalk; in west Kent a glauconitic sandstone, the **Upper Greensand**, appears between the Gault and the Chalk. The Upper Greensand thickens westwards as the Gault thins, so that in Hampshire and the Isle of Wight they are about equal, in Dorset the Upper Greensand is much thicker than the Gault and finally in mid-Devonshire there is no Gault, only Upper Greensand. The Upper Greensand and Gault are shown by their ammonites to be of the same age and the conditions of sandy, as distinct from clayey, deposition must have spread gradually eastwards during this span of time. The marine transgression which carried the Gault sea over the London landmass is also clearly seen in south-west England,

where the Upper Greensand rests unconformably on the eroded edges of the Jurassic and Triassic strata between Dorset and Dartmoor (Fig. 28).

The Chalk

The advance of the sea continued with the deposition of the **Chalk**. This is in general a soft, pure, fine-grained limestone, deposited in a uniform clear sea into which very little land-derived sand or clay was carried. Only around the extreme margins of the Chalk are there signs of passage into sandy deposits, indicating approach to land. In the lower part of the Chalk, such sandy marginal beds are found in Wiltshire, Dorset and Devonshire, but later the sea advanced still further and the marginal deposits of the Middle Chalk and the lower part of the Upper Chalk are now to be found (in Britain) only in northern Ireland. Finally the sea reached its maximum extent in the latter part of Upper Chalk times, patches of Upper Chalk which have escaped erosion being found now in the Hebrides and south-west Ireland.

This maximum marine advance – the most complete disappearance of the land beneath the sea for which there is evidence in the whole British geological record – was apparently followed by rapid regression. The evidence for this comes mainly from the other side of the North Sea basin, in Denmark, where the typical Upper Chalk is followed by shallow-sea limestones which pass up into Tertiary clays and sands. In Britain this

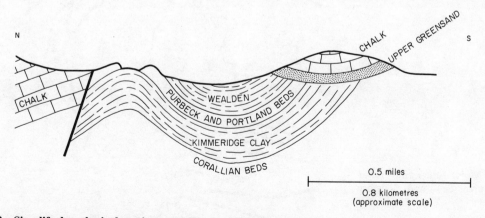

Figure 28 Simplified geological section near Weymouth, Dorset
The Jurassic and Wealden beds were folded and eroded in Lower Cretaceous times and the Upper Greensand and Chalk were then deposited unconformably upon their eroded edges. The Upper Greenland and Chalk were later themselves folded and faulted.

evidence of regression was destroyed because the Chalk was folded and eroded at the end of the Cretaceous, and the Tertiary beds rest unconformably upon it.

Cretaceous plate movements

The Cretaceous is also important as the period in which the European and North American crustal plates, which had been joined by the Caledonian orogeny, began to drift apart again to form the present Atlantic Ocean. Major faulting produced graben structures to the west of what is now Ireland and these widened progressively as the North American plate began to move westwards. The rifts cut across the Caledonian and Armorican fold lines so that some parts of these were left in Europe while other parts moved with North America (Fig. 12, p. 15). So the new Atlantic sea (it did not become an ocean until oceanic-type crust was formed in it, probably in late Cretaceous times) was not in the same position as the old Iapetus ocean of the Lower Palaeozoic. (The earliest marine sediments in the Atlantic are actually Jurassic but most of the initial splitting of Europe from North America, and also of Africa from South America, took place during the Cretaceous.) The incoming of the Lower Greensand sea into southern England marks an important phase in this creation of an Atlantic seaway.

During the same period extensive rifting of the crust took place in the North Sea (Fig. 29) and it seems almost a matter of chance that the main separation of the crustal plates occurred west of Ireland and not between Great Britain and the European continent. Otherwise Britain might now be part of America.

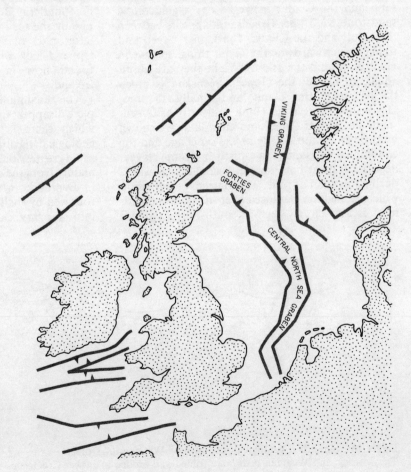

Figure 29 Major faults and graben of the North Sea and Western Approaches

Tertiary cycles of sedimentation and igneous activity

The Cretaceous/Tertiary boundary is the only division between eras in the British post-Cambrian succession which is not bound up with a period of mountain-building. For one thing the British area was a long way from the Mesozoic geosyncline and hence from the orogenic folding of it (the Alpine mountain-building, Ch. 13), so was not directly involved as it was with the Caledonian and Armorican orogeneses. But perhaps a more important point is that the vast Cretaceous marine transgression, which was worldwide, followed by the abrupt regression which ushered in the Tertiary, had a catastrophic effect upon the life of the time. At least it seems reasonable to ascribe to that cause the changes in fauna which make Cretaceous and Tertiary (or **Cenozoic**) as clearly distinct, in their fossil content, as any other two eras. The ammonites and belemnites, the great sea reptiles (ichthyosaurs, plesiosaurs, mosasaurs) and several other characteristic Mesozoic groups of animals were quite suddenly extinguished at the end of the Cretaceous. On the land, the dinosaurs died out and left the field free for the rapid expansion of the mammals during the Tertiary. There was also a big change in plant life – the true flowering plants, including grasses, spread and became dominant in the Tertiary. However, this was a much less dramatic change which had begun well back in the Cretaceous.

During the Lower Tertiary (Eocene and Oligocene) the sea was generally present in the English Channel and Western Approaches and, very importantly, in the North Sea basin. The latter was a subsiding basin in which a thick continuous series of sediments, mainly clays, accumulated. From this basin, the sea periodically flooded over the south-east quarter of England (and likewise over Holland and Belgium and parts of the Paris Basin), each advance of the sea being followed by a retreat. The strata outcropping in onshore Britain thus contain evidence of several **cycles of sedimentation**: marine beds (the transgressive phase) followed by non-marine (the regressive phase) and then marine again. At least eight such cycles are recognisable in the Eocene

and Oligocene of southern England, providing a useful way of subdividing the beds.

Tertiary sediments in southern England

The many deep wells which have been drilled down to the Chalk beneath London (Fig. 31) provide evidence of the first two of these cycles. Resting unconformably on the Chalk is the **Thanet Sand**, a marine deposit, showing the sea coming in over the eroded land surface of the Chalk. Above come the **Woolwich Beds**, which are here semi-marine lagoonal. The Woolwich Beds are marine sands in east Kent, while west of London they are non-marine deltaic sands and clays (the so-called Reading Beds). Thus the Thanet Sand sea had retreated again to complete the cycle, giving a picture in Woolwich Beds times of a large delta spreading from the west (Reading Beds), fringed along the coast by semi-marine lagoons (the London Woolwich Beds) and passing eastwards into a shallow sea (east Kent Woolwich Beds). The **London Clay**, which comes above, is a thick and completely marine clay formation, representing a fresh deepening and incursion of the sea and the beginning of the next cycle.

Higher strata (Claygate and Bagshot Beds) can be seen capping the hills around London, and higher still (Bracklesham and Barton Beds) in Hampshire and the Isle of Wight. These are, in general, sands and clays, alternately marine and non-marine, and all belong to the **Eocene** period, the main characteristic of which is that marine horizons are more extensive and numerous than non-marine. The opposite is the case with the **Oligocene** strata, which are mainly lacustrine and deltaic with only thin marine bands. The typical freshwater molluscs *Viviparus* and *Unio* appear frequently in the Oligocene, along with other freshwater fossils which sometimes make up shelly lacustrine limestones very much like those of the Purbeck and the Weald Clay. At Bovey Tracey, Devonshire, is a large outlier of completely

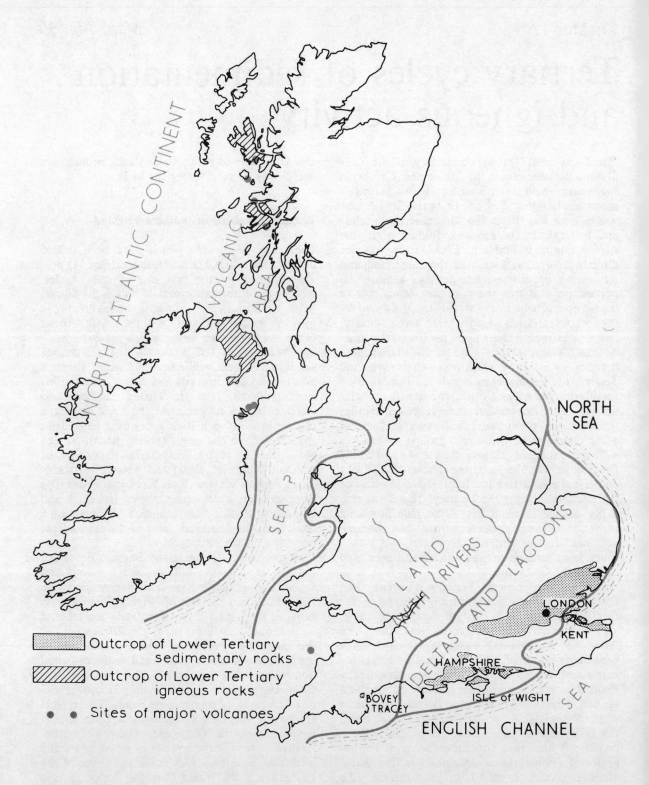

Figure 30   Outcrops of Lower Tertiary rocks and the geography of Lower Tertiary times
At times the area shown here as 'deltas and lagoons' was submerged beneath the sea. The rivers are diagrammatic only, but the sites of volcanoes are well documented.

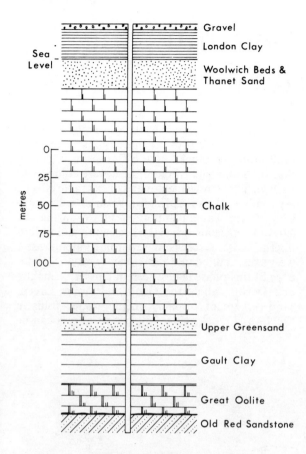

Figure 31 A borehole under London
Note the great unconformity between the Jurassic and the Upper Palaeozoic, and the absence of nearly all the Mesozoic below the Gault. The London Clay happens to be very thin, owing to erosion, in central London where this borehole was drilled; elsewhere in the London Basin it is much thicker.

freshwater lake clays. All these beds indicate a general retreat of the sea.

Only the lower part of the Oligocene is represented in Britain, and even that is confined to the Isle of Wight and the opposite mainland coast (apart from outliers in Dorset and Devon). This is because of the Alpine folding which, about the end of Oligocene times, folded and uplifted the beds and led to severe erosion.

Tertiary igneous activity

Meanwhile in western Scotland and northern Ireland Eocene rocks of a totally different type had been formed. This region was the site of intense volcanic activity at this time, and the positions of seven or eight great volcanoes, on the scale of the Hawaiian volcanoes of the present day, have been traced. These emitted vast quantities of lava, mainly basalt, which still cover considerable areas. Associated with the volcanic activity was the intrusion of masses of granite and gabbro and also of dense swarms of dykes, some of which can be traced across to the north-east coast of England. Interbedded with the lavas are some sediments, including poor coal seams and clays with plant remains, but no sign of marine influence. Similar activity was then going on in what are now the Faroe Islands and Greenland. It was at this time that the Atlantic split between the European and American plates was extending northwards from the British area towards the Arctic. All this North Atlantic volcanic activity is symptomatic of the uprise of magma associated with a passive plate margin.

The Alpine mountain-building and the later Tertiary

After the Carboniferous, no geosynclinal rocks were formed in Britain. The European geosyncline during the Mesozoic was a complex one situated approximately along the line of the Mediterranean and the Alps, and occupied by the geosynclinal sea known to geologists as Tethys. This geosyncline underwent several preliminary folding movements, culminating in a main phase in the middle or late Oligocene when the Alpine fold mountains were formed.

The British area was a long way from the margins of the geosyncline and from the direct effects of the orogeny. Nevertheless the compression of Tethys into the Alps, together with the widening of the Atlantic which was going on at the same time, resulted in the pushing about of great fault-bounded blocks of the European crust, so that the sediments lying on them were folded and faulted. These movements had considerable effects, especially in the south English basin of sedimentation. There was an important phase during the Lower Cretaceous, when the beds up to and including the Lower Greensand were folded along east–west axes, faulted and subsequently eroded. Evidence of this phase is best seen in Dorset, Wiltshire and Devon, where the Gault and Upper Greensand rest unconformably on the eroded folds in the Jurassic rocks (Fig. 28), but its effects can be

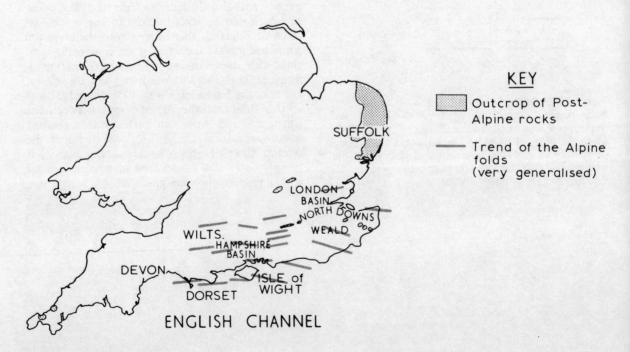

Figure 32   Alpine structures

traced further east. A second marked phase came at the end of the Cretaceous, when the Chalk was folded, uplifted and eroded, so that the basal Tertiary beds are now found to rest upon different parts of the Chalk in different places. The effects of this second phase are also seen in the Hebrides, where the Chalk was folded and faulted before the extrusion of the Eocene basalts.

The effects of the main late Oligocene phase are seen most clearly in Dorset, the Isle of Wight, central southern England and the Weald region, where all the beds up to and including the Oligocene are strongly folded – spectacularly so along the Dorset coast and in the Isle of Wight – and also faulted. The general style of the structures is of a swarm of short parallel anticlines, mostly asymmetric, with a steep northern limb and gentler southern limb. They trend very approximately east–west but are **en echelon**, that is each anticline is offset from its nearest neighbour. The scale of the folding is shown by the fact that the main asymmetric anticline of the Isle of Wight (often wrongly called a monocline) has an amplitude of nearly 1250 metres. On a still broader scale, the main anticlinorial upfold of the Weald and synclinorial downfolds of the London and Hampshire basins date chiefly from this time, although their development apparently started during the post-Chalk, pre-Tertiary movements. In Britain, outside the area where Cretaceous and Tertiary rocks occur at the present day, there is plenty of evidence that the Mesozoic rocks have been gently folded and, especially, faulted. Probably most of these structures were produced by the Oligocene movements.

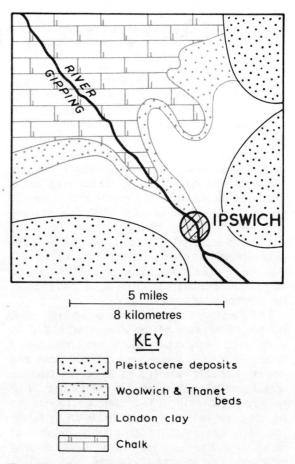

Figure 33 The Alpine unconformity
Sketch-map of part of Suffolk, showing how the Pleistocene deposits lie unconformably upon the Lower Tertiary and Cretaceous as a result of the Alpine mountain-building movements.

Post-Alpine deposition

The Oligocene folding and faulting, and the general uplift associated with it, virtually put an end to deposition within the area that is now the land of Britain. There are almost no sediments at all to represent the latter part of the Oligocene, the whole of the **Miocene** and most of the Pliocene – a period of some 30 million years. This was entirely a land period, with erosion, not deposition, going on (as, of course, it has been and continues to be over a large part of Britain since the Cretaceous). Miocene and Pliocene sediments were deposited in the North Sea and Irish Sea basins and the English Channel. In fact, by this time the geography was almost modern – the north Atlantic was present as an Ocean in place of the old northwestern landmass, the volcanic land of Eocene times having broken up and drifted apart. In the **Pliocene**, the North Sea, as it can now be called, sometimes flooded the land margin to deposit traces of shallow sea sediments which can be found in Suffolk (the Coralline Crag) and along the North Downs. Similar deposition continued in the early part of the **Pleistocene** (for example, the Red Crag of East Anglia).

The Quaternary glaciations

The Quaternary era, in which we are now living, started about 1½ million years ago. There is little real justification for separating it from the Tertiary Era, since its only really distinctive feature is the occurrence of the great Pleistocene glaciations. The equally severe glaciations of earlier times, such as are known to have occurred in the late Precambrian and the Permian, are not regarded as justifying the erection of separate eras. Likewise the usual convenient division of the Quaternary into the Pleistocene period, during which the glaciations occurred, and the Holocene, or Postglacial period, is artificial since there is no proof that the so-called 'postglacial period' of the present day is not merely an interglacial, and that the ice will not advance again.

The glaciations took the form of several major periods of advance of the glaciers separated by long, mild interglacial periods. At least one of these interglacials lasted some 200 000 years and was considerably warmer than the present climate, with hippopotamuses living in the Thames. It is usually considered that four main glaciations can be recognised in Europe, separated by interglacials, but each was itself made up of a number of advances and retreats and thus is more correctly regarded as a group of glaciations.

There is no evidence of any actual glacial activity in Britain during the first of these four groups, when only the higher mountains of Europe were affected. During this time marine sediments were being deposited in eastern England, as mentioned in Chapter 13 (the Red Crag and Icenian Crag of East Anglia and some scattered deposits around the London Basin). These, like the sediments deposited in other parts of Europe unaffected by the glaciers, are dated as Pleistocene rather than Pliocene on the evidence of their fossils, especially the presence of bones and teeth of the true horse and the true elephant. These latter fossils were washed into the sea from the nearby land surface, but the marine fossils themselves give evidence that the climate was becoming colder, since there is a marked increase in species which normally live nearer the Arctic, and a decrease in southern species. The same kind of change in plant life is shown by study of the wind-blown pollen grains found in the sediments.

The glaciation of Britain

The next two groups of glaciations were those that had the most widespread effects in Britain. Ice sheets spread out from the main centres of glacier accumulation, namely the Scottish Highlands, Southern Uplands, Lake District, North Wales and the mountains of Donegal and Connemara. In addition, the huge ice sheet spreading from the Scandinavian mountains crossed the North Sea at times and impinged upon eastern England. The main effects of glaciation in the highland areas from which the ice came were of erosion, all the well known features of ice-eroded mountains being visible in these districts.

The ice sheets also spread out over the lowlands, reaching at their maximum extent the Thames Valley, the Cotswolds and the north coast of Devon and Cornwall. Here their main effect was depositional, laying down variable thicknesses of **till** (boulder clay), fringed by moraines and by masses of outwash sands and gravel carried away from the ice by meltwater streams. South of the area actually glaciated was a region of periglacial semi-desert, like the tundra regions of northern Canada and north Siberia today. Here the effects of permanently frozen subsoil are often very noticeable even today, especially the **head** deposits caused by the weathered surface layers sliding down hill during the melting season over the permanent ground-ice below – a process known as **solifluction.**

The growth and shrinkage of the ice sheets led to marked oscillation in the levels of both land and sea. The rivers therefore, were alternately depositing alluvial gravels derived from the load of debris brought down by the glaciers, and eroding their beds through these gravel deposits to leave remnants of them as **river terraces**. Raised beaches and submerged forests along the coasts show that sea level rapidly oscillated.

Evidence for the advances and retreats of the ice sheets lies especially in the alternation of these characteristic deposits. Ideally a boulder clay (glaciation) is overlain by outwash sands (retreat of the ice sheet), then either lake deposits may come, or the boulder clay is eroded by a river which forms river terraces (interglacial period).

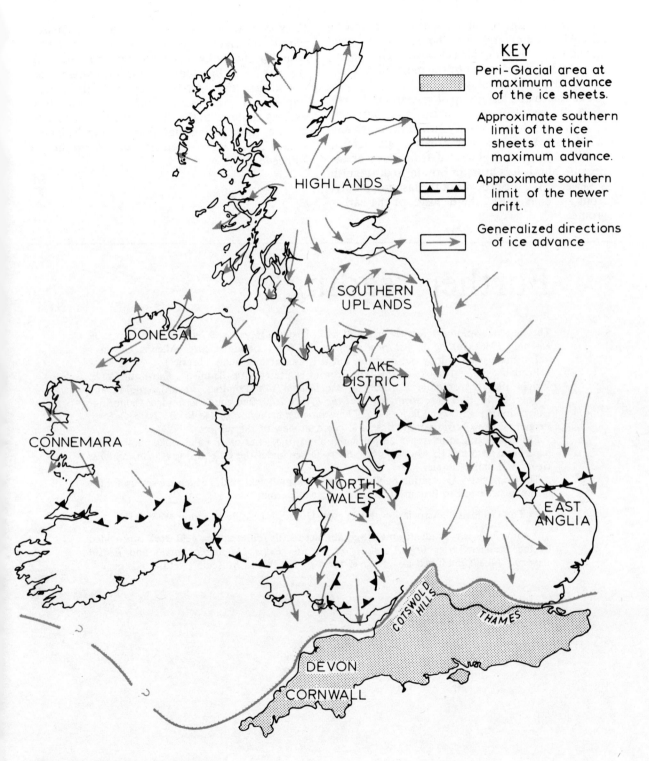

KEY

Peri-Glacial area at maximum advance of the ice sheets.

Approximate southern limit of the ice sheets at their maximum advance.

Approximate southern limit of the newer drift.

Generalized directions of ice advance

HIGHLANDS

SOUTHERN UPLANDS

LAKE DISTRICT

DONEGAL

CONNEMARA

NORTH WALES

EAST ANGLIA

COTSWOLD HILLS

THAMES

DEVON

CORNWALL

Figure 34   The Quaternary glaciations

These are overlain by solifluction deposits (return of cold climate) and then boulder clay again (glaciation), the underlying deposits being sometimes folded and churned by the mechanical force of the advancing ice mass.

The fourth and last group of glaciations did not reach the centre or south of England; but their effects are much more clearly seen in the north and in Wales than those of the earlier glaciations, which they largely obliterated from these areas. Because of this it is usual in Britain to distinguish a 'newer drift', the deposits of the last group only, from an 'older drift', the deposits of the earlier groups.

Finally, it must be remembered that the Quaternary is the era of the development of man. *Homo* would probably be a suitable indicator fossil for the base of the Pleistocene if only his remains were not so rare. Fortunately the trace fossils of man, implements, are less rare, but they appear to be entirely confined to the Pleistocene and Holocene, short as those periods have been on the geological scale. There is no evidence of *Homo* in the Pliocene.

Further reading

The best one-volume reference book of British stratigraphy is: Wells, A. K. and J. F. Kirkaldy 1966. *Outline of historical geology*, 5th edn (London: George Allen & Unwin – unfortunately this is long out of print, but it is available in many libraries).

Probably the best books of this type in print at present are: Bennison, G. M and A. E. Wright 1969. *The geological history of the British Isles* (London: Edward Arnold); and Rayner, D. H. 1981. *The stratigraphy of the British Isles*, 2nd edn (Cambridge: Cambridge University Press). Owen, T. R. 1976. *The geological evolution of the British Isles* (Oxford: Pergamon Press) gives a more dramatic personal view of the subject.

For more detailed reference on particular areas, the series of 18 handbooks published in paperback form by Her Majesty's Stationery Office under the general title *British Regional Geology* is indispensable.

The Geologists' Association publishes a series of small field guides which are vey useful for planning fieldwork in Britain. These are obtainable from:

The Geologists' Association, Burlington House, Piccadilly, London W1V OJU.

A convenient way of identifying the commoner fossils found during field work is provided by the excellent series *British Palaeozoic Fossils*, *British Mesozoic Fossils* and *British Cenozoic Fossils* published in soft-cover form by the British Museum (Natural History).

Index

Numbers in italics refer to text figures.

INDEX